The Cult of Ignorance

A thought-provoking exploration of fanaticism and the value of critical thinking

Robin Jackson

North Star Publishing
99 Pitcairn Road
Durban
4001
South Africa

For The Curious

CONTENTS

Introduction

Ignorance is not a passive absence of knowledge; it is an active force, a stubborn refusal to engage with ideas that challenge our comfort zones, beliefs, or worldviews. It is not simply "not knowing"; it is the celebration of "not needing to know." This book is a response to that dangerous phenomenon, which Isaac Asimov so aptly described in his 1980 essay, A Cult of Ignorance. Asimov's observations remain startlingly relevant today, particularly in a world where misinformation flourishes, anti-intellectualism thrives, and critical thinking is dismissed as elitism.

But this book is not just about societal ignorance; it is also personal. I write these words as someone who once inhabited a world governed by certainty and unquestionable truths, a religious cult. For years, my life revolved around dogma. Every aspect of my existence was dictated by doctrines handed down from supposed authorities, and questioning those teachings was not only discouraged but considered outright rebellion. Escaping that environment was one of the hardest and most illuminating journeys of my life.

It was through that process of awakening that I came to understand the true power of critical thinking and the profound dangers of fanaticism. Reflecting on Isaac Asimov's essay, I found echoes of my own experiences in his critique of society's glorification of ignorance. He wrote, *"There is a cult of ignorance in the United States, and there always has been. The strain of anti-intellectualism has been a constant thread winding its way through our political and cultural life, nurtured by the false notion that democracy means that 'my ignorance is just as good as your knowledge.'"*

This quote hit me like a revelation. The "cult of ignorance" Asimov described was not just a societal trend; it was a mindset I knew intimately. It is a mindset that thrives not only in religious or political circles but also in everyday interactions. It is the dismissal of expertise, the distrust of intellectuals, the comfort of simplistic answers over uncomfortable truths. It is the refusal to engage with complexity because complexity requires effort, humility, and the willingness to admit we might be wrong.

This book, then, is both a warning and a call to action. It is a warning about the dangers of a world where ignorance is celebrated and intellectualism is vilified. But it is also a call to embrace curiosity, critical thinking, and the courage to question. These are qualities that have the power to break down the walls of fanaticism and build bridges to understanding.

My Journey from Certainty to Curiosity

Before exploring the broader themes of this book, let me

share a little about my own journey. I grew up in an environment that claimed to have all the answers. The group I was part of—some would call it a religion, others a cult—offered a ready-made worldview. It gave me purpose, community, and certainty. But it also demanded conformity. Independent thought was dangerous, questions were discouraged, and doubt was treated as a personal failing. For years, I accepted this framework. It was comforting to believe that the world could be neatly divided into good and evil, right and wrong, truth and falsehood. But as I grew older, cracks began to form. I started to notice inconsistencies in the teachings, hypocrisies among the leaders, and questions that no one seemed willing to answer.

The turning point came when I began to read books and articles from outside the group's approved material. It was a terrifying act of rebellion. One that filled me with guilt at first. But it also opened my eyes to a world of ideas I had never considered. One of those ideas was the importance of critical thinking.

Critical thinking is not just about solving problems or making decisions. It is about cultivating intellectual humility. The ability to say, "I don't know," and then seek answers. It is about recognizing the limits of our own knowledge and being willing to listen to those who know more. It is about valuing evidence over emotion, logic over loyalty, and truth over tribalism.

This was not an easy lesson to learn. Leaving the group meant losing my community, my identity, and my sense of certainty. It meant confronting uncomfortable truths about myself and the world. But it also meant gaining something far more valuable: the freedom to think for myself.

The Cult of Ignorance in Society

What I experienced on a personal level is mirrored in society at large. Just as I once lived in a bubble of certainty, insulated from challenging ideas, many people today inhabit echo chambers where their beliefs are never questioned. Social media algorithms reinforce these bubbles, feeding us content that aligns with our existing views and shielding us from opposing perspectives.

This phenomenon is not new. As Asimov noted, the cult of ignorance has deep roots in history. From the persecution of Galileo for daring to suggest that the Earth revolves around the sun to the Scopes Monkey Trial, which pitted evolution against creationism, anti-intellectualism has always found ways to assert itself. What has changed in recent years is the speed and scale at which ignorance can spread.

The internet, for all its benefits, has become a double-edged sword. It provides access to unprecedented amounts of information, but it also enables the rapid dissemination of misinformation. Conspiracy theories, pseudoscience, and "alternative facts" can gain traction faster than the truth. The result is a society where expertise is devalued, and the line between opinion and fact becomes increasingly blurred.

This is dangerous for many reasons, but perhaps the most insidious is how it erodes trust in institutions. Scientists, educators, and journalists, who dedicate their lives to the pursuit of knowledge, are often dismissed as elitist or out of touch. In their place, we see the rise of self-proclaimed "experts" whose primary qualifications are their ability to confirm what people want to believe.

Why Critical Thinking Matters

At its core, this book is about the antidote to ignorance:

critical thinking. Critical thinking is not just a skill; it is a mindset. It is the willingness to question, to doubt, to challenge, and to learn. It is the courage to face uncomfortable truths and the humility to admit when we are wrong.

But critical thinking is not easy. It requires effort, discipline, and a willingness to engage with complexity. It requires us to resist the allure of simple answers and to confront the biases that shape our perceptions. And it requires us to value knowledge for its own sake, even when it does not serve our immediate interests. Asimov understood this well. In his essay, he lamented the tendency of society to equate democracy with the idea that all opinions are equally valid. "The strain of anti-intellectualism," he wrote, "has been nurtured by the false notion that democracy means that 'my ignorance is just as good as your knowledge.'"

This is a profoundly dangerous idea. Democracy depends not on the equal validity of all opinions but on the equal opportunity to participate in informed decision-making. When ignorance is celebrated, democracy is undermined. When expertise is dismissed, progress is stalled.

A Call to Action

The cult of ignorance is not an inevitable phenomenon. It is a choice, a choice made by individuals, communities, and societies. And like any choice, it can be changed. This book is my contribution to that change. It is an invitation to question, to doubt, and to think. It is a challenge to reject the comfort of certainty and embrace the uncertainty of learning. It is a reminder that the pursuit of knowledge is not a luxury; it is a necessity.

In the chapters that follow, we will explore the forces

that sustain ignorance and the strategies needed to overcome it. But for now, let me leave you with this thought: ignorance is not just a lack of information; it is a lack of curiosity. And curiosity, the desire to know, to understand, to grow, is the antidote to ignorance.

This book is for the curious. If you have ever felt frustrated by the prevalence of misinformation, disheartened by the dismissal of expertise, or inspired by the power of a good question, then this book is for you. Let us embark on this journey together, not as a lecture but as a conversation. A conversation about the value of thinking, the dangers of fanaticism, and the power of curiosity to transform our lives and our world.

Chapter 1

The Origins of Anti-intellectualism

'I'm tired of ignorance held up as inspiration, where vicious anti-intellectualism is considered a positive trait, and where uninformed opinion is displayed as fact." — Phil Plait

Ignorance is often dismissed as a personal failing, but in reality, it is a carefully cultivated social condition. It does not survive in isolation; it flourishes within systems designed to sustain it. To grasp the roots of anti-intellectualism; which is defined as the deliberate mistrust of intellectuals, critical thought, and expertise; we must first ask: why is ignorance so seductive?

The hostility toward knowledge is nothing new. History is littered with moments when society turned against its thinkers. Socrates was sentenced to death for "corrupting" Athenian youth, Galileo was condemned for affirming a heliocentric universe, and countless others have been silenced, exiled, or worse for speaking inconvenient truths. These episodes are often treated as exceptions, but they are part of a recurring pattern, one in which intellectual progress is met with resistance from the very structures it threatens.

At its core, anti-intellectualism is rooted in fear. Fear of change, fear of complexity, fear of losing control. To those in power, intellectualism is dangerous. It questions authority, challenges norms, and demands accountability. To the general public, it can feel alienating, its language and concepts distant from everyday concerns. Faced with these discomforts, many choose to reject rather than engage, preferring the reassuring simplicity of ignorance over the unsettling weight of knowledge.

The Roots in Religious Dogma

The early seeds of anti-intellectualism can be traced back to religious institutions, which often positioned themselves as the sole arbiters of truth. In medieval Europe, the Church held dominion over knowledge, branding certain ideas as heretical and punishing anyone daring enough to challenge them. This period was defined by a strict hierarchy of knowledge: the clergy stood at the top as intermediaries to divine truth, while the common person was expected to accept without question.

Galileo Galilei's trial serves as a telling example. His assertion that the Earth revolved around the Sun wasn't merely a scientific theory, it was an outright challenge to the Church's authority. By questioning the geocentric model, Galileo threatened the religious cosmology that upheld the Church's power. His punishment was not a matter of error but of defiance. It was a challenge to the very order that had long been enforced.

During the Enlightenment, thinkers like Voltaire and Rousseau championed reason and education, yet their ideas were met with fierce resistance from those who saw intellectualism as a threat to tradition and control. Similarly, in 19th-century America and Europe, populist movements often framed intellectuals as out-of-touch elites, championing instead the wisdom of the "common man."

Voltaire, a staunch critic of both the Catholic Church and absolute monarchy, famously declared, "I may disapprove of what you say, but I will defend to the death your right to say it." His works, particularly Candide, satirized the irrationality of blind faith and the injustices sustained by unchecked power. Likewise, Jean-Jacques Rousseau, more focused on the social contract and humanity's inherent goodness, argued for the importance of education in shaping moral and rational individuals. His treatise *Emile* outlined a revolutionary approach to education that emphasized natural development and critical thought over rote memorization and rigid discipline.

For the Catholic Church, the Enlightenment's emphasis on reason and skepticism was a direct challenge to its theological and moral authority. Monarchs and aristocrats, whose power often rested on divine right or hereditary privilege, feared that the spread of Enlightenment ideas would incite rebellion among the masses. Their resistance was far from passive. It manifested in censorship, persecution, and violence. Voltaire himself was exiled and imprisoned multiple times for his writings, while Rousseau's works were banned and burned across several nations. The tension between Enlightenment ideals and traditional power structures highlighted an age-old theme: the clash between progress and preservation, between the pursuit of knowledge and the maintenance of control.

This historical pattern reveals a truth: institutions that fear losing power often suppress intellectual progress.

But religion is not the sole culprit. Similar dynamics emerge in political, economic, and cultural spheres, where the threat of new ideas is met with resistance.

The Democratization of Ignorance

With the Enlightenment came the promise of liberation through knowledge. Universal education, the scientific method, and democratic ideals were heralded as the pillars of progress. Yet, this very democratization of knowledge gave rise to an ironic paradox: the democratization of ignorance.

In today's world, the internet has revolutionized how we access and share information. Unlike previous generations, who relied on books, newspapers, and other traditional media, modern individuals can instantly tap into an ocean of information with just a few clicks. This unprecedented access has democratized knowledge, empowering people from all walks of life to educate themselves on virtually any subject.

However, not all information is created equal. The internet, while a powerful tool for education and communication, also nurtures misinformation, conspiracy theories, pseudoscience, and "alternative facts." This duality exposes a deeper societal issue: the failure to adequately teach critical thinking, which is crucial for navigating the complexities of the digital age.

The internet undeniably serves as a repository of human knowledge. Platforms like Wikipedia, online academic journals, and educational websites make it easier than ever to find reliable information. A student researching World War II can, in mere minutes, access peer-reviewed articles, primary source documents, and expert analyses. Similarly, professionals in various fields can stay up to date on industry developments through online courses, webinars, and forums. This accessibility offers an unprecedented opportunity for lifelong learning and personal growth.

Yet, the internet's open nature also makes it a breeding ground for misinformation. Anyone with an internet connection can publish content, regardless of its accuracy or credibility. This has led to the rise of conspiracy theories, such as the flat Earth movement, which has made a shocking resurgence due to viral videos and social media posts. Similarly, pseudo-scientific claims about health, such as the anti-vaccine movement, have gained ground despite being debunked by the scientific community. The spread of "alternative facts," a term popularized by political figures to describe misleading or false information, further complicates the landscape, blurring the line between truth and fiction.

This proliferation of misinformation reflects a broader societal failure to teach critical thinking. Critical thinking, the ability to objectively analyze and evaluate information, is essential for forming reasoned judgments. It requires skills such as questioning assumptions, recognizing biases, and discerning credible sources. Yet these skills are often neglected in educational systems, which prioritize rote memorization and standardized testing over analytical thinking. As a result, many are ill-equipped to critically assess the information they encounter online.

Addressing this problem demands a multi-faceted approach. First and foremost, there must be a greater emphasis on teaching critical thinking skills in schools. This means integrating critical thinking into curricula across all subjects, from science to history, literature to mathematics. Students should be encouraged to question, evaluate evidence, and consider multiple perspectives. For instance, a history lesson on the Civil

War could prompt discussions on how different sources portray its causes and consequences, teaching students to analyze biases and motivations behind each account.

Alongside formal education, media literacy must become a vital skill in the digital age. Media literacy—understanding how information is produced, distributed, and consumed—is crucial for navigating today's information landscape. It involves distinguishing between news and opinion, identifying credible sources, and understanding the role algorithms play in shaping online content. Public awareness campaigns and community programs can help promote media literacy, empowering individuals to become more discerning consumers of information.

Technology companies also bear responsibility for addressing the spread of misinformation on their platforms. This includes refining algorithms to prioritize credible sources, flagging misleading content, and providing tools for users to report misinformation. Social media platforms, in particular, wield significant influence over the spread of information, and must take active steps to curb the dissemination of falsehoods.

In a surprising move, Meta, the parent company of Facebook, Instagram, and Threads, has announced major changes to its content moderation policies. Founder Mark Zuckerberg revealed in a video titled *"More Speech, Fewer Mistakes"* that Meta would eliminate its reliance on fact-checking organizations, opting instead for a community notes system similar to X (formerly Twitter). This system allows users to flag and annotate posts they believe to be misleading or false. Zuckerberg argued that fact-checking organizations are biased and often censor rather than promote informed discourse. He emphasized Meta's commitment to free speech, particularly on sensitive topics like gender and immigration. These changes will apply across Meta's platforms, which serve over 3 billion users worldwide.

In addition to this policy shift, Meta plans to move its content moderation teams from California to Texas. Zuckerberg claims this will reduce perceived bias and help build trust, though some experts suspect political motivations behind the move, especially with the upcoming U.S. presidential election. Samuel Woolley, a propaganda researcher, suggested that this relocation aligns with Texas's political climate, which is seen as more supportive of conservative values than California. This move mirrors actions by Elon Musk, who relocated Tesla's headquarters to Texas, citing California's policies on gender identity notifications in schools as a motivating factor.

The policy changes raise concerns about the spread of misinformation, as the community notes system relies on user input rather than professional fact-checkers. Critics fear that this system could lead to inconsistent moderation and the amplification of false or harmful content. However, the long-term effects of these shifts remain unclear, particularly in how they will influence the quality of information and public discourse online.

This failure to foster critical thinking has profound implications. Misinformation has the power to shape public opinion, influence political discourse, and even impact public health. Without proper tools for discerning truth from falsehood, society risks undermining its very foundations.

Cultural Shifts Toward Anti-Intellectualism

In recent decades, cultural attitudes toward intellectualism have undergone a dramatic shift. The rise of consumerism and celebrity worship has given birth to a new hierarchy of values, where fame and wealth often eclipse knowledge and expertise. Celebrities and influencers are seen as more relatable and trustworthy than academics or scientists, leading to the devaluation of intellectual pursuits.

This shift is further fueled by the rise of reality TV and infotainment, which prioritize entertainment over substance. Shows like Keeping Up with the Kardashians and The Jerry Springer Show glorify drama and sensationalism, while sidelining critical thinking and intellectual curiosity. The result is a culture that values ignorance over knowledge, where emotional reasoning replaces evidence-based decision-making.

The Consequences of Anti-Intellectualism

The consequences of anti-intellectualism are far-reaching and profound. It erodes trust in institutions and expertise, weakening the very foundations of democracy and governance. In public health, anti-intellectualism has led to unnecessary illness and death. On a global scale, rejecting scientific consensus on issues like climate change hampers progress and exacerbates the challenges humanity faces.

The long-term effects on society are equally concerning. By devaluing knowledge and expertise, anti-intellectualism fosters a culture of cynicism and disengagement. It becomes harder to address collective challenges and build a more equitable and sustainable future.

Chapter 2

THE WORSHIP OF IGNORANCE

Humility and knowledge in poor clothes excel pride and
ignorance in costly attire.
- William Penn

We live in an era of unparalleled access to information, yet ignorance has become a badge of honor. The dismissal of expertise, the celebration of "common sense" over critical analysis, and the elevation of uninformed opinions above evidence-based reasoning are not just cultural quirks; they are symptoms of a larger crisis. Isaac Asimov's warning about the "cult of ignorance" is more relevant than ever. What was once seen as a deficiency to overcome has now been reframed as a virtue, weaponized to sow division and distrust in institutions that once anchored society.

The Myth of the "Everyman" and the Rejection of Expertise

The romanticisation of the "common man" as a beacon of innate wisdom has deep roots in Western thought. Thomas Paine's "Common Sense" championed the idea that ordinary people could challenge the complexities of governance, which was an empowering notion in its time. But that principle has since been distorted into a justification for outright rejection of expertise.

This idealization manifests in media, politics, and everyday culture. The phrase "ignorance is bliss" encapsulates a broader narrative that equates a lack of knowledge with purity or innocence. In popular media, idyllic portrayals of rural life or childhood nostalgia often frame ignorance as a form of moral superiority. But in the real world, this mindset has far more troubling consequences.

Modern politics has taken this distortion to new heights. The self-styled "outsider" politician, rejecting intellectualism in favour of folksy, relatable rhetoric, has become a staple of contemporary populism. Figures like Donald Trump in the United States and Jair Bolsonaro in Brazil have capitalized on public resentment toward perceived elitism, portraying their own lack of expertise as a virtue. Trump dismissed climate science as a "hoax," pushed unproven COVID-19 treatments, and reveled in his defiance of expert consensus. Bolsonaro downplayed COVID-19 as a "little flu" while railing against lockdowns, leading to catastrophic consequences for Brazil.

The Media's Complicity in the Celebration of Ignorance

If ignorance has become a commodity, the media is one of its most effective distributors. Reality TV, social media, and partisan news networks all play a role in amplifying uninformed voices. The illusion of balance, where every viewpoint is given equal weight regardless of merit, creates a dangerous false equivalency. A scientist with decades of experience is pitted against a conspiracy theorist, and viewers are left to "decide for themselves."

Conservative media outlets have made an industry out of attacking intellectuals. Talk show hosts like Rush Limbaugh and Tucker Carlson have spent years painting experts as detached, self-serving elites, reinforcing the idea that knowledge itself is suspect. Even well-intentioned media figures have contributed to the problem. The Oprah Winfrey Show and The Dr. Oz Show have given platforms to pseudo-scientific claims, fueling skepticism toward vaccines and legitimate medicine. In 2009, Oprah gave Jenny McCarthy; who is a vocal anti-vaccine activist; a massive stage to spread misinformation, contributing to a wave of vaccine hesitancy that still lingers today.

Ignorance as a Political Tool

Ignorance is not just a personal failing; it has become a deliberate political strategy. Slogans like "trust your gut" and "common sense over science" are not just rallying cries, they are calculated attempts to undermine expertise and rational discourse. Brexit campaigners in the UK dismissed economic warnings from experts as "Project Fear," persuading voters to reject facts in favor of emotion.

Meanwhile, underfunded education systems contribute to the problem by prioritizing rote memorization over critical thinking. A 2018 study by the Reboot Foundation found a decline in critical thinking skills among U.S. students, linking it to an overemphasis on standardized testing. If future generations cannot discern credible information from misinformation, the cycle of ignorance will only intensify.

The Digital Age: Amplifying Misinformation

Social media, once heralded as a democratizing force for information, has instead become a breeding ground for ignorance. Algorithms prioritize engagement over accuracy, rewarding sensationalism and conspiracy theories over well-researched facts. Facebook, for example, played a central role in spreading COVID-19 misinformation. A 2021 study found that just 12 anti-vaccine accounts were responsible for 65% of anti-vaccine content on the platform. Despite efforts to curb misinformation, these accounts continued to thrive, undermining public health efforts worldwide.

The Consequences of Worshiping Ignorance

The consequences of this cultural shift are not abstract, they are deadly. The following are examples of how deadly it can be.

The Anti-Vaccine Movement:

Despite overwhelming scientific evidence supporting vaccines, misinformation has led to declining vaccination rates and the resurgence of preventable diseases. The 2019 measles outbreak in Samoa, which resulted in over 5,700 cases and 83 deaths, was fueled by anti-vaccine propaganda.

As I write this (February 2025), Texas and New

Mexico are experiencing a significant measles outbreak, with 99 confirmed cases across both states. The outbreak, described as the largest in decades for Texas, has primarily affected unvaccinated individuals and is centered in Gaines County.

Climate Change Denial:

Organizations like the Heartland Institute, backed by fossil fuel interests, have systematically spread climate misinformation, delaying action on a crisis that threatens global stability.

The Politicization of COVID-19:

Trump's endorsement of hydroxychloroquine, despite a lack of scientific support, led to mass confusion and a rush for an ineffective treatment. The rejection of masks and vaccines turned a public health crisis into a political battlefield, costing lives in the process.

How Do We Reverse This Trend?

The celebration of ignorance is not inescapable. It is the product of systemic failings, including those in education, media responsibility, and political debate. Reversing it requires a collective effort.

Schools must move beyond standardized testing and equip students with the ability to evaluate information critically. Ethical journalism must take precedence over sensationalism. News outlets must resist the temptation to give equal weight to misinformation in the name of "balance."

The public must be educated on how to navigate the information age, recognizing misinformation and understanding how algorithms shape their worldview. We must challenge the notion that expertise is elitist and instead promote intellectual curiosity as a civic virtue.

The Fight Against the Cult of Ignorance

This is not just a cultural annoyance; it is a direct threat to democracy, public health, and global progress. When ignorance is elevated above knowledge, when gut feelings replace evidence, and when expertise is treated as a liability rather than an asset, societies suffer. The fight against ignorance is not about shaming those who lack knowledge but about restoring a culture that values learning, curiosity, and the pursuit of truth. Only then can we build a future that is informed, resilient, and capable of facing the challenges ahead.

Chapter 3

The Myth of Equal Opinions

Opinion is the medium between
knowledge and ignorance.
- Plato

The idea that "every opinion matters" has become a sacred tenet in a society that prides itself on equality. But somewhere along the way, this noble ideal has been distorted into a dangerous fallacy: the belief that all opinions are equally valid, regardless of evidence, expertise, or logic. This misconception not only erodes critical thinking but also allows ignorance to masquerade as informed debate. The consequences are far-reaching, influencing political discourse, public health, scientific progress, and the very fabric of rational decision-making.

The Roots of the Myth

The notion that all opinions deserve equal weight stems from a core democratic principle: the right to free speech. Democracy, at its heart, is built on the premise that every individual has an equal voice in shaping governance and society. However, this principle is often misapplied in contexts where knowledge and expertise should take precedence over uninformed conjecture. John Stuart Mill, in his seminal work On Liberty, argued for the importance of free speech and open debate, not as an endorsement of all opinions as equal, but as a mechanism for refining truth. His "Mill's Trident" framework outlines three key justifications for free expression:

- We may be wrong: Free speech allows others to correct our errors.

- We may be partially correct: Opposing viewpoints help us refine our understanding.

- We may be entirely correct: Defending our views against challenges strengthens our grasp of the truth.

Mill insisted that the pursuit of truth requires continuous confrontation with error. Falsehoods and flawed ideas, when properly scrutinized, serve a vital role in reinforcing knowledge. He warned that suppressing dissenting opinions, even erroneous ones, leads to intellectual stagnation. As he put it, "All silencing of discussion is an assumption of infallibility."

He emphasized that it is harmful for several reasons:

- It assumes infallibility: "All silencing of discussion is an assumption of infallibility."

- It robs humanity of potential truths: We may be mistaken, and suppressing an opinion could deprive us of discovering a truth.

- It weakens our grasp of truth: Even if an opinion is false, engaging with it strengthens our understanding of why the truth is true.

The Danger of Unchallenged Beliefs

Mill warned against the complacency that comes with unchallenged beliefs. He argued that without constant scrutiny and debate, even true beliefs can become "dead dogmas" rather than "living truths." This lack of engagement leads to a superficial understanding of one's own positions and a failure to grasp their full implications.

The Marketplace of Ideas

Mill's philosophy laid the groundwork for the concept of the "marketplace of ideas," where free expression allows the best ideas to emerge through competition and scrutiny. However, it's important to note that Mill's understanding of speech was primarily focused on the assertion of truth-apt propositions and the pursuit of knowledge.

Limitations and Modern Challenges

While Mill's arguments remain influential, they face challenges in the modern context, particularly with the rise of social media:

- Not all speech aims at truth: Mill's focus on

truth-seeking doesn't always apply to modern forms of expression.

• Information overload: The sheer volume of information and opinions can make it difficult for truth to emerge naturally.

• Echo chambers: Social media algorithms can reinforce existing beliefs rather than facilitating genuine debate.

Despite these challenges, Mill's core insight remains relevant: the importance of fostering an environment where ideas can be freely expressed, challenged, and refined. As he eloquently put it, "Truth gains more even by the errors of one who, with due study and preparation, thinks for himself, than by the true opinions of those who only hold them because they do not suffer themselves to think."

In modern discourse, this assumption has eroded. The democratic value of equality has been stretched to suggest that every opinion, no matter how uninformed or unfounded, deserves equal consideration. This has led to the rise of a false equivalence in public debates, where the weight of evidence is sidelined in favour of giving equal airtime to opposing views, regardless of their merit.

False Equivalence in Public Debate

Somewhere along the way, the democratic principle of free speech was twisted into a false equivalence: the assumption that all opinions are equally valid, no matter how uninformed. This fallacy has poisoned public debate, particularly in areas where expertise is crucial, such as climate science, medicine, and public policy.

Take climate change as an example. The overwhelming consensus among scientists is that human activity is driving global warming. Yet, public discourse often presents this as a "debate," giving equal weight to climate scientists and climate change deniers. The result? A manufactured controversy that confuses the public and delays meaningful action.

A similar phenomenon occurred during the COVID-19 pandemic. Public health experts, armed with decades of research, found themselves battling misinformation from individuals who believed their social media "research" was just as credible. The phrase "Do your own research" became a rallying cry for anti-vaccine movements, highlighting the dangerous conflation of access to information with actual expertise.

The Role of Social Media

Social media has exacerbated this problem by leveling the playing field between experts and amateurs, fact and fiction. Platforms like Facebook, Twitter, and YouTube provide a megaphone to anyone, enabling misinformation to spread at an unprecedented rate. Worse, social media algorithms prioritize engagement over accuracy, amplifying sensationalism while burying nuanced, evidence-based arguments.

A study by MIT researchers found that false news spreads 70% faster than the truth. In this digital landscape, a climate scientist and a conspiracy theorist appear equally credible to the casual observer. Expertise is drowned in a sea of noise, where the loudest voices, rather than the most informed, dominate. In these digital spaces, the line between expertise and opinion becomes blurred. A climate scientist with decades of experience can share the same platform as a conspiracy theorist, and to the casual observer, their arguments may appear equally credible.

The Dunning-Kruger Effect

The persistence of uninformed opinions can, in part, be explained by the Dunning-Kruger effect, a cognitive bias in which individuals with limited knowledge overestimate their understanding. Someone with a rudimentary grasp of virology might confidently dismiss vaccines simply because they misunderstand how they work. Worse, when these individuals find like-minded communities online, their misconceptions are reinforced, emboldening them to challenge experts with unwarranted certainty.

The Dunning-Kruger effect reveals a fundamental flaw in the myth of equal opinions: confidence is not competence. Expertise matters. Without it, people are more likely to mistake their own ignorance for insight.

The Danger of "Opinionism"

This cultural devaluation of expertise has fueled an era of "opinionism," the belief that personal opinions are sufficient to engage in debates about complex issues. This mindset dismisses facts and expertise as secondary to belief. It is particularly dangerous when it seeps into public policy, where decisions must be grounded in reality, not populist sentiment.

Consider the anti-mask and anti-vaccine movements. Politicians, pandering to public opinion rather than expert advice, contributed to public health crises. When leadership prioritizes the whims of the uninformed over the guidance of specialists, society suffers the consequences.

Moving Beyond the Myth

To combat the false equivalence of opinions, society must reaffirm the value of expertise. This does not mean silencing dissent, but it does mean recognizing that not all opinions are equally valid. Some are simply wrong.

Education is the first line of defense. Schools must emphasize critical thinking, teaching students to differentiate between informed arguments and baseless assertions. Media literacy programs should equip individuals to navigate misinformation and discern credible sources from unreliable ones.

Journalists and public figures have a responsibility to challenge false equivalence. Not every issue has "two sides." When the evidence overwhelmingly supports one position, presenting a misleading "balance" only serves to obscure the truth.

Politicians must resist the temptation to pander to populist sentiments at the expense of informed decision-making.

A Call for Intellectual Humility

Ultimately, dismantling the myth of equal opinions requires a commitment to intellectual humility, which is the ability to recognize the limits of one's knowledge and defer to those with greater expertise when appropriate. It means fostering a culture where admitting uncertainty is seen as a strength, not a weakness.

The belief that all opinions are equally valid may seem democratic, but it is, in reality, deeply destructive. By placing uninformed opinions on the same pedestal as expert analysis, society weakens its ability to confront complex challenges. The path forward necessitates a fresh commitment to evidence, expertise, and intellectual humility—principles that will guide the discussions in the coming chapters.

Chapter 4

Media & Misinformation

All I know is just what I read in the papers, and that's an alibi
for my ignorance. - Will Rogers

In an era of limitless information, one would expect society to be more informed than ever. Yet, the opposite seems true. The sheer volume of knowledge has resulted in confusion rather than enlightenment, as disinformation, whether conveyed intentionally or unintentionally, continues to contaminate public debate.

Isaac Asimov's warning about the "cult of ignorance" is as relevant as ever, as media institutions, which should ideally inform, scrutinize power, and foster understanding, often serve as the primary conduit for ignorance. This chapter dissects how misinformation flourishes in modern media, how manipulation steers public opinion, and what happens when a society loses its ability to distinguish fact from fiction.

The Israel-Palestinian Conflict: A Case Study in Media Misinformation

Few geopolitical conflicts have been as distorted by media narratives as the Israel-Palestinian struggle. Mainstream media outlets, whether through prejudice, oversimplification, or outright propaganda, have played an important role in shaping, and frequently misrepresenting, public opinion.

The conflict, with its deep historical, religious, and political roots, is frequently reduced to sensationalist headlines that prioritize immediate events over historical context. The British Mandate, the 1948 Arab-Israeli War, and the Six-Day War of 1967 are often ignored in favour of a click-worthy crisis of the moment. The result? A fractured, misinformed public, with each side clinging to media narratives that reinforce their pre-existing biases.

The Israel-Palestinian conflict is a stark reminder of the media's power to shape public perception and influence global events. By perpetuating bias, oversimplification, and false narratives, mainstream media contributes to the spread of misinformation and the deepening of divisions. Responsible reporting, grounded in accuracy, context, and fairness, is essential to fostering a more informed and balanced understanding of this complex and deeply consequential conflict.

The Myth of White Genocide in South Africa: Unravelling a Dangerous Narrative

In recent years, the claim of a "white genocide" targeting farmers in South Africa has gained traction in certain circles, particularly among right-wing groups and on social media platforms. This narrative has been amplified by high-profile figures like Elon Musk and former U.S. President Donald Trump, sparking international debate and concern. However, a closer examination of the facts reveals that this claim is not only unsupported by evidence but also serves to distort the complex realities of crime, land reform, and racial dynamics in post-apartheid South Africa.

The Origins of the Myth

The concept of a "white genocide" in South Africa has its roots in the country's complex history of racial inequality and the ongoing process of land reform. Following the end of apartheid in 1994, the South African government has been working to address the stark disparities in land ownership that resulted from centuries of discriminatory policies.

As of 2025, approximately 72 percent of agricultural land in South Africa is still owned by white farmers, despite white South Africans making up less than 9% of the population. This imbalance has led to ongoing debates about land redistribution and reform, which have sometimes been mischaracterized or exaggerated by those opposed to such changes.

The Role of Crime Statistics

One of the primary arguments used to support the "white genocide" narrative is the claim that white farmers are being disproportionately targeted in violent attacks. However, a careful analysis of crime statistics tells a different story.

According to Africa Check, a fact-checking organization, white South Africans are actually less likely to be murdered than any other racial group in the country. While whites account for nearly 9% of the South African population, they represent just 1.8% of murder victims.

Lizette Lancaster from the Institute for Security Studies has stated that "Whites are far less likely to be murdered than their black or coloured counterparts." This is further supported by data showing that murder rates in predominantly white suburbs of Johannesburg are significantly lower than in black townships.

Farm Attacks in Context

While farm attacks are a serious concern in South Africa, it's crucial to understand them within the broader context of crime in the country. South Africa has one of the highest crime rates globally, affecting all areas and population groups.

Lynsey Chutel, a South African journalist, reported in 2018 that after peaking in 2001/2002, the number of farm attacks had decreased to about half. Similarly, murders on farms peaked in 1997/1998 at 153 but had fallen below 50 by 2018.

More recent data shows that between July 2017 and July 2018, 47 farmers of all races were killed in South Africa, down from 66 in the previous year. To put this in perspective, there were a total of 19,016 murders in South Africa between April 2016 and March 2017, indicating that farmers are not exceptionally likely to be victims of homicide.

Motivations Behind Farm Attacks

While some farm attacks may have racial motivations, experts argue that the primary drivers are economic rather than racial. Gareth Newham, who leads the justice and violence prevention program at the Institute for Security Studies in South Africa, explains that white farmers are likely targeted due to their relative wealth and vulnerability in remote areas, rather than their race.

"Far-right groups in South Africa actively travel to America and promote this white genocide narrative because, naturally, in a country with a high murder rate, white individuals are also victims," Newham notes, adding that the murder rate among white individuals is lower compared to other racial groups.

The Spread of Misinformation

The "white genocide" narrative has been particularly persistent on social media platforms, where it has found a receptive audience among white nationalists and far-right groups. This online ecosystem has allowed the myth to spread rapidly, often divorced from factual context.

In August 2023, Elon Musk, the South African-born CEO of Tesla and Twitter (now X), tweeted, "They are openly pushing for genocide of white people in South Africa." Such high-profile endorsements of this narrative, despite lacking factual basis, have given it unwarranted credibility and reach.

Political Implications

The myth of white genocide in South Africa has had significant political implications, both domestically and internationally. In the United States, it has been used as a rallying cry by white nationalist groups and has influenced foreign policy discussions.

In 2018, then-President Donald Trump tweeted about "land and farm seizures and expropriations and the large scale killing of farmers" in South Africa, instructing his Secretary of State to investigate. This tweet was widely seen as an endorsement of the white genocide conspiracy theory and caused diplomatic tension between the U.S. and South Africa. In February 2025, Trump mirrored his 2018 rhetoric when he cut aid to South Africa following the signing of the Expropriation Act.

The Reality of Land Reform

The fears surrounding land reform in South Africa have been a key factor in fueling the white genocide myth. However, the reality of land reform efforts is far more nuanced than the alarmist narratives suggest

South African President Cyril Ramaphosa has emphasized that land reform will be carried out in a legal and orderly manner, without undermining agricultural production or food security. The Expropriation Act, which has been a source of controversy, is designed to address historical injustices while maintaining economic stability. The misrepresentation has been that expropriation has never occurred and that the ANC intends to conduct Zimbabwe-style land grabs, which is simply not accurate.

Debunking the Myth

Numerous fact-checking organizations, academic institutions, and international bodies have thoroughly debunked the notion of a white genocide in South Africa. Africa Check, a respected fact-checking organization, has consistently rejected these claims as false. Gregory Stanton of Genocide Watch, while acknowledging that "early warnings of genocide are still deep in South African society," has explicitly stated that "genocide has not begun". Stanton has also condemned the misuse of his organization's reports to further the idea of white genocide.

The persistence of the white genocide myth is not merely a matter of misinformation; it has real and dangerous consequences. By framing South Africa's complex social and economic challenges through a racial lens, it exacerbates tensions and hinders efforts at reconciliation and equitable development.

Moreover, the myth trivializes the experiences of other South Africans who face high rates of violent crime. As one analysis points out, "Given that poorer Black people are disproportionately at risk of violence, the insistence that Whites face a planned and intentional genocide on the basis of their race invisibilizes and trivializes other victims of violence in South Africa."

The myth of white genocide in South Africa is a dangerous fabrication that distorts the realities of crime, land reform, and racial dynamics in the country. While South Africa certainly faces significant challenges, including high crime rates and the need for equitable land distribution, there is no evidence to support claims of a targeted campaign against white farmers.

As South Africa continues to grapple with the legacy of apartheid and works towards a more equitable society, it is crucial that discussions about these issues are grounded in facts rather than inflammatory rhetoric. The persistence of the white genocide myth not only misrepresents the situation in South Africa but also threatens to undermine efforts at reconciliation and social progress.

In the words of Joe Walsh, a British journalist who investigated these claims, "If there was any kind of genocide being carried out against white people in the country then the safest areas of the continent's most dangerous city would not be predominately white." This statement encapsulates the fundamental flaw in the white genocide narrative and underscores the importance of critically examining such claims.

As we move forward, it is essential to promote a nuanced understanding of South Africa's challenges, one that acknowledges the country's complex history while working towards a more just and equitable future for all its citizens, regardless of race.

The Evolution of Media

To understand the role of media in perpetuating ignorance, we must first examine its evolution. In the early 20th century, mass media was limited to newspapers, radio, and eventually television—centralized institutions that required significant resources to produce and distribute content. While these media outlets were not immune to bias, they operated under journalistic standards that prioritized fact-checking and editorial oversight.

The advent of the internet and social media upended this dynamic. Platforms like Facebook, Twitter, and YouTube democratized content creation, allowing anyone with an internet connection to publish their ideas to a global audience. While this democratization has empowered marginalized voices and expanded access to information, it has also eroded traditional gatekeeping mechanisms. In this new media ecosystem, accuracy often takes a backseat to engagement, clicks, and shares.

The Algorithm Problem

At the heart of modern media manipulation lies the algorithm. Social media platforms and search engines use complex algorithms to determine what content users see.

These algorithms are designed not to inform but to maximize engagement, often by promoting content that triggers emotional responses such as anger, fear, outrage, or joy. As a result, sensationalism thrives. Fake news stories, conspiracy theories, and polarizing content frequently outperform factual reporting. A 2018 study by MIT found that false news spreads six times faster on Twitter than true stories. This is not merely a coincidence; misinformation is often designed to be emotionally gripping and easily shareable, making it inherently more "viral" than nuanced, evidence-based reporting.

The impact of these engagement-driven algorithms extends beyond just social media platforms. Search engines also use similar principles, potentially affecting the visibility of different types of content across the internet. This algorithmic bias towards engaging content over factual accuracy poses significant challenges for information dissemination and public discourse in the digital age.

The Misinformation Epidemic

Misinformation is not a new phenomenon, it has been a tool of propaganda for centuries. However, its scale and impact have been amplified in the digital age. Social media platforms provide fertile ground for the spread of falsehoods, which can range from harmless myths to dangerous lies.

One of the most striking examples of modern misinformation is the anti-vaccine movement. Despite overwhelming scientific evidence supporting the safety and efficacy of vaccines, misinformation linking vaccines to autism has persisted for decades. This false claim originated from a discredited study published in 1998 and has since been perpetuated through social media, leading to vaccine hesitancy and the resurgence of preventable diseases like measles.

The COVID-19 pandemic further highlighted the deadly consequences of misinformation. From false cures to conspiracy theories about the virus's origins, misinformation undermined public health efforts and sowed distrust in institutions. A study published in The Lancet estimated that vaccine misinformation contributed to thousands of preventable deaths worldwide.

Manipulation in the Media

Misinformation is not always accidental. In many cases, it is a deliberate tool of manipulation. Political actors, corporations, and even foreign governments exploit media platforms to shape public opinion and advance their agendas.

In the early 2000s, major media outlets, particularly in the United States and the United Kingdom, widely reported that Iraq possessed weapons of mass destruction (WMDs). This claim was based on faulty intelligence and was amplified by government officials, leading to widespread public support for the U.S.-led invasion of Iraq in 2003. The Bush administration, along with major news organizations like The New York Times and Fox News, repeated these claims without sufficient scrutiny.

And what were the consequences? No WMDs were ever found in Iraq, exposing the misinformation that justified the war. The invasion led to the deaths of hundreds of thousands of Iraqis, the displacement of millions, and long-term regional instability. It contributed to the rise of extremist groups like ISIS, which emerged from the power vacuum left by the war. Additionally, public trust in the media and government eroded significantly, fueling skepticism toward official narratives.

Political propaganda is one of the most common forms of media manipulation. In democratic societies, politicians and interest groups use misinformation to sway voters and discredit opponents.

For example, during the 2016 U.S. presidential election, Russian operatives used social media to spread divisive content, targeting specific demographics with tailored messages. Using fake social media accounts and groups posing as Americans, such as "Heart of Texas," they spread false narratives portraying Hillary Clinton as corrupt and promoting Donald Trump as a savior of American values.

These efforts included divisive content targeting racial tensions, immigration, and political ideologies, often using sensationalist imagery and language to amplify engagement This strategy, known as micro-targeting, leverages data analytics to exploit individual biases and fears, making it a powerful tool for manipulation.

The impact was far reaching and swift. The campaign exacerbated political polarization in the U.S., deepening societal divides along racial and ideological lines. It undermined trust in democratic institutions and electoral processes, with many Americans questioning the legitimacy of the election outcome. Additionally, the misinformation spread by these campaigns continues to fuel conspiracy theories, such as QAnon, which have had lasting effects on American politics.

Corporate interests also play a significant role in shaping media narratives. Public relations campaigns often blur the line between advertising and journalism, creating "advertorials" that disguise promotional content as unbiased reporting. Industries with vested interests, such as fossil fuels and tobacco, have historically used media manipulation to downplay the risks associated with their products, delaying regulatory action and public awareness.

The Decline of Trust

One of the most insidious effects of misinformation and manipulation is the erosion of trust. As the public becomes increasingly aware of the prevalence of fake news and biased reporting, trust in media institutions has plummeted. According to a 2021 Gallup poll, only 36% of Americans expressed a "great deal" or "fair amount" of trust in mass media, the lowest level in decades.

This decline in trust creates a feedback loop: as people become more skeptical of mainstream media, they turn to alternative sources, many of which lack credibility or accountability. These echo chambers reinforce pre-existing beliefs and deepen societal divisions, making it even harder to establish a shared understanding of reality.

The Role of Confirmation Bias

Another aspect that contributes to media-driven ignorance is confirmation bias, or the inclination to seek out information that supports one's own opinions. In an age of information overload, people often gravitate toward sources that confirm their worldview, ignoring evidence that contradicts it. Social media platforms exacerbate this problem by creating "filter bubbles," where algorithms show users content similar to what they have previously engaged with.

Over time, these bubbles insulate individuals from diverse perspectives, reinforcing biases and making it harder to engage in constructive dialogue. Addressing the challenges posed by media, misinformation, and manipulation requires a multifaceted approach. Teaching individuals how to critically evaluate sources, identify misinformation, and fact-check claims is essential. Media literacy programs should be integrated into school curricula and promoted through public awareness campaigns.

Social media platforms must be held accountable for the role their algorithms play in spreading misinformation. Policy-makers can advocate for transparency in how algorithms function and push for regulations that prioritize accuracy over engagement. Fact-checking organizations play a crucial role in debunking misinformation and promoting accurate reporting.

Encouraging collaboration between journalists, academics, and tech companies can strengthen these efforts. Investing in independent, evidence-based journalism is critical for countering misinformation. Governments, philanthropists, and the public can support trustworthy news outlets through funding, subscriptions, and donations. Encouraging civil dialogue and fostering spaces for constructive debate can help bridge divides and counteract the polarizing effects of misinformation.

While the challenges posed by media manipulation and misinformation are daunting, they are not insurmountable. By fostering media literacy, demanding accountability from tech companies, and supporting quality journalism, society can begin to reclaim the media as a force for truth and understanding.

Chapter 5

Ignorance on the Silver Screen

There's never been a noble war except in the history books and propaganda movies. - Harold G. Moore

Like so many of us, I like to curl up on the couch with a bag of popcorn to watch a good movie or series every so often. But beneath the glitz and glamour of Hollywood there often lies a more insidious reality: the film industry's long-standing role as a purveyor of propaganda and perpetuator of ignorance. From its early days to the present, Hollywood has frequently aligned itself with political and military agendas, shaping public opinion through the power of cinema.

The Military-Entertainment Complex

Since World War II, the Pentagon has recognized cinema's power to shape public perception. Blockbusters like Top Gun (1986), with its sleek fighter jets and high-octane bravado, and Zero Dark Thirty (2012), which turned the search for Osama bin Laden into a gritty procedural, do more than entertain; they sanitise war. These films benefit from military cooperation, gaining access to cutting-edge equipment, personnel, and technical expertise. But there's a price: scripts are vetted and often rewritten by the Department of Defense's Film Liaison Office to ensure the military's image remains pristine. This isn't mere collaboration, it's soft censorship.

The trade-off is clear. Films that align with the Pentagon's preferred narrative get blockbuster budgets and glossy realism. Those that challenge militarism, like Platoon (1986) or Born on the Fourth of July (1989), are denied support, forced to work around Hollywood's powerful gatekeepers. The result? A cultural landscape dominated by recruitment-ready propaganda: war as noble, soldiers as untouchable heroes, dissent as unpatriotic noise.

Supporters argue that military input ensures accuracy, but that's a red herring. Accuracy isn't the objective; propaganda is. When the Pentagon scrubs sexual assault from Crimson Tide (1995), minimizes civilian casualties in Iron Man (2008), or downplays the devastation of nuclear war in Godzilla (2014), it's not refining realism; it's manufacturing consent. These films do more than just entertain; they also pacify, hiding the moral difficulties of war—drone strikes, torture, imperial overreach—and portraying warfare as clean, essential, and just.

The consequences are real. When Hollywood becomes an amplifier for the Pentagon, it doesn't just shape movies, it shapes public opinion. Studies show military-themed entertainment bolsters recruitment and fosters unquestioning support for interventionist policies. In an era of endless war, this kind of storytelling has serious repercussions: a desensitized public, an unchecked military-industrial complex, and a democracy eroded by state-sanctioned narratives.

This isn't a call to ban military collaborations; it's a demand for transparency. Audiences deserve to know when the Pentagon has shaped their entertainment, and filmmakers must resist the lure of military backing if it means compromising artistic integrity. True art thrives in dissent, not deference.

At its best, cinema challenges, provokes, unsettles. But as long as Hollywood remains tethered to the Pentagon, its most impressive illusion will be the one that hides the truth: war isn't heroic, and it certainly isn't entertainment.

Perpetuating Stereotypes and Ignorance

Hollywood has always been a master storyteller, crafting narratives that shape how the world sees itself. However, for Arab and Muslim populations, the business has rarely served as a mirror, but rather as a grotesque distortion, a funhouse reflection that reduces entire cultures to vulgar stereotypes. For decades, Western audiences have been fed the same tired images: the menacing terrorist, the oppressive sheikh, the veiled woman longing for liberation. This isn't just lazy storytelling; it's cultural propaganda with real-world consequences.

From the silent film era to modern blockbusters, Hollywood has wielded its influence to frame Arabs and Muslims as exotic curiosities at best and existential threats at worst. Aladdin (1992) painted a fictionalized "Agrabah" as a land of barbarism and spectacle, while True Lies (1994) turned Arab villains into snarling, bomb-strapped caricatures. After 9/11, this trend accelerated. Shows like 24 and films like The Kingdom (2007) relentlessly conflated Islam with violence, cementing the false equivalence between faith and fanaticism in the public imagination. These portrayals don't merely misinform; they stoke fear, fueling policies that treat entire communities as security threats.

The damage is measurable. Studies show that media representations shape public perception and policy. In the years following 9/11, discrimination, harassment, and hate crimes against Arab and Muslim Americans surged. Hollywood didn't invent anti-Muslim sentiment, but it certainly amplified it. When the only roles available to Arab and Muslim actors are villains, victims, or voiceless background figures, the message is clear: their stories don't matter unless they serve Western narratives.

Defenders of these stereotypes frequently rely on arguments such as "artistic license" or "reflecting real-world fears." But these justifications don't hold up. Hollywood's depiction of Arabs and Muslims isn't about realism; it's about control. These characters are rarely granted inwardness or complexity. They exist to menace, intrigue, or be vanquished. Meanwhile, white savior narratives like American Sniper (2014) reinforce the myth of Western moral superiority, portraying the Middle East as a lawless wasteland in need of American intervention.

Then there's Hollywood's other favored trope: exoticism. Films like Sex and the City 2 (2010) present Arab cultures as lavish, mysterious backdrops, where camels roam beside gleaming skyscrapers and veiled women exist only to be pitied. These portrayals reduce entire civilizations to set pieces, stripping them of their contemporary realities, their diversity, their humanity.

To its credit, Hollywood has made some progress. Shows like Ramy and Ms. Marvel have proven that authentic, nuanced storytelling resonates with audiences.

But these are the exceptions, not the rule. For every The Night Of (2016), which offers a rare, humanizing portrayal of a Muslim protagonist, there's Homeland (2011–2020), perpetuating the same old Islamophobic tropes. Token representation is not enough; systemic change is required.

The solution? Power must shift. Arab and Muslim creatives need to be more than just "consultants." They need to be the ones telling their own stories, without Hollywood's filter. Studios must stop greenlighting scripts that recycle harmful tropes and start investing in narratives that reflect reality, not outdated fears. And audiences must demand better, rejecting stories that trade in bigotry for box office appeal.

Hollywood's stereotypes aren't just offensive, they're dangerous. When an industry with global influence repeatedly reduces a people to villains and victims, it doesn't just distort reality; it fuels prejudice, shapes policy, and endangers lives. Until Hollywood confronts its role in this cycle, its legacy will remain not one of storytelling, but of complicity.

Hollywood's Invisible Hand: The Power of Soft Propaganda

Hollywood has long positioned itself as an apolitical dream machine, a place where audiences can escape the weight of reality. But this is a carefully crafted illusion. For more than a century, the entertainment industry has been a master of stealth, slipping ideological messaging into its stories under the guise of harmless entertainment. Hollywood does more than merely reflect culture; it also constructs it, planting ideas before viewers are aware they have been sold a belief.

Elmer Davis, the head of the U.S. Office of War

Information during World War II, summed it up best: propaganda is most effective when disguised as entertainment. Consider the wartime films of the 1940s, such as Casablanca (1942) and Mrs. Miniver (1942), which combined patriotic fervour with romance and drama. Audiences came for the love stories, the suspense, the intrigue. But they left with a reinforced belief in Allied moral superiority and the necessity of war. The propaganda wasn't in the script; it was in the subtext, absorbed effortlessly.

This playbook hasn't vanished, it just evolved. Today's blockbusters, from Top Gun: Maverick (2022) to the Marvel Cinematic Universe's militarized superhero narratives, follow the same blueprint. These films don't bludgeon audiences with overt messaging; they seduce them with high-octane aesthetics. Fighter jets streaking across the sky in golden-hour lighting, charismatic soldiers delivering quippy one-liners, and war framed as an exhilarating adventure. The Pentagon's fingerprints are all over these productions—offering funding, access to military hardware, and script "guidance." By the time viewers recognize the recruitment-ad undertones, they've already internalized the message: America's military might is righteous, war is heroic, and questioning either is unpatriotic. What makes this kind of "soft propaganda" so effective is its subtlety. Unlike state-sponsored films or overt political messaging, Hollywood's narratives are cloaked in neutrality. They entertain first, persuade second.

A superhero movie isn't about militarism, it's about saving the world. A sci-fi thriller isn't about surveillance, it's about cool technology. But by positioning military alliances as essential to heroism or portraying mass surveillance as a necessary evil, these films normalize dangerous ideologies. They render complex issues—

perpetual war, privacy erosion, xenophobia—into background noise, unworthy of serious thought.

The consequences are profound. When messaging is packaged as entertainment, critical thinking takes a backseat. Audiences don't question the ethics of drone warfare when it's presented as a thrilling action sequence. They don't push back against Islamophobic stereotypes when every terrorist in an action film speaks in a heavy accent and clutches a prayer bead before detonating a bomb. Soft propaganda doesn't argue, it assumes. It replaces debate with emotion, making ideology feel instinctive rather than imposed.

Some might argue that audiences are sophisticated enough to separate fiction from reality. But psychology says otherwise. Studies show that even when people recognize fictional bias, repeated exposure still shapes their beliefs. The "mere exposure effect" ensures that the more we see something, whether it's a noble soldier or a Middle Eastern villain, the more we accept it as truth. Hollywood's global reach magnifies this effect: these stories don't just shape American perspectives; they shape how the entire world views power, justice, and identity.

This isn't to say all entertainment is propaganda. Films can challenge power just as easily as they reinforce it. Parasite (2019) and Get Out (2017) prove that mainstream cinema can provoke deep, unsettling thought. But these are the exceptions in an industry that overwhelmingly rewards narratives that align with institutional interests. For every subversive hit, there are a dozen Pentagon-approved action flicks, fossil fuel-backed studio projects, and algorithm-driven productions designed to avoid anything "controversial" (read: anything that questions authority).The solution isn't to demonize Hollywood, it's to demand transparency and media literacy.

Viewers deserve to know when their favorite blockbusters are shaped by government or corporate interests. Imagine if every military-backed film carried a disclaimer: This movie was produced with U.S. Department of Defense oversight. Schools should be teaching students how to dissect the politics of their favorite franchises, understanding that even apolitical stories carry ideological weight. And filmmakers must resist the lure of institutional backing when it means sacrificing truth for access.

Hollywood's soft propaganda is one of democracy's most insidious threats. By masking ideology as entertainment, it bypasses our critical defenses, turning film into a tool of manipulation. In an age where misinformation is everywhere, the most dangerous lies aren't the ones we recognize. They're the ones we don't even realize we've absorbed. Until we confront the invisible hand shaping our screens, the stories we love will keep shaping worldviews we never consciously chose.

The Responsibility of Filmmakers: Authenticity vs. Soft Propaganda

Hollywood has always been in the business of shaping reality. It doesn't just tell stories, it manufactures worldviews, reinforcing some narratives while erasing others. The push for diversity in film, often dismissed as "too woke," isn't about political correctness or forced inclusivity. It's about dismantling an industry that has long functioned as a well-oiled machine of cultural conditioning. The real question isn't whether Hollywood should embrace diversity, but whether it can do so without falling into the same propagandistic tendencies that have shaped its past.

For over a century, Hollywood has dictated public perception, frequently in ways that serve power rather than truth. From early Westerns that glorified Manifest Destiny to Cold War-era films that painted communism as an existential threat, the industry has never been a passive storyteller. Government agencies, particularly the military and intelligence sectors, have played a direct role in shaping these narratives, providing funding, resources, and script approval to ensure that Hollywood's version of reality aligns with strategic interests. The result? An entertainment landscape where certain voices are amplified, others are distorted, and some are erased entirely.

Diversity in filmmaking, then, isn't just a matter of representation, it's a matter of storytelling integrity. Audiences don't just consume movies; they absorb their underlying assumptions. If a film about war presents soldiers as unquestioned heroes while ignoring the civilian cost, that's not entertainment, it's an advertisement. If Hollywood churns out cop dramas that frame law enforcement as infallible, that's not storytelling, it's PR. The industry's challenge is to embrace diversity not as a trend but as a corrective measure, an effort to tell richer, more honest stories that reflect the world as it is, rather than as certain institutions wish it to be.

Recent successes like Everything Everywhere All At Once and Abbott Elementary prove that authentic, nuanced storytelling resonates. These works don't just insert diversity for diversity's sake; they craft stories where representation isn't an afterthought but an essential element. Compare this to the more superficial approach, in which diversity is seen as a marketing tool, and studios, while congratulating themselves on casting a diverse lead, continue to greenlight films driven by the same old power structures.

Filmmakers today have a responsibility beyond just filling quotas. They must challenge Hollywood's ingrained biases, question the narratives that have been historically favored, and resist the lure of institutional backing that comes at the cost of truth. True diversity means not only casting underrepresented groups but also ensuring that the writers, directors, and producers shaping these stories come from varied backgrounds and perspectives. It means breaking away from the well-worn formulas designed to avoid controversy, because too often, "controversy" is just another word for uncomfortable truths.

But the burden doesn't fall solely on filmmakers. Audiences, too, must engage critically with what they consume. We must recognize that no film exists in a vacuum. Every story has a political dimension, whether explicit or not. When Hollywood presents war as clean and justified, or police brutality as a necessary evil, we should ask: Who benefits from this framing? Who is being silenced?

The goal isn't to make every film a political statement. It's to acknowledge that films already are. The fight for diversity in Hollywood is not about erasing history or pushing an agenda; it's about expanding the conversation. It's about recognizing that the narrow, sanitized version of reality that Hollywood has long presented is itself an agenda—one that has gone largely unchallenged.

Filmmakers stand at a crossroads: they can either continue reinforcing the industry's historical biases or break the cycle, pushing for stories that are not just entertaining but also honest. The choice isn't about being "woke." It's about being real. And if Hollywood wants to remain relevant in a world that is more connected and aware than ever, it must stop treating diversity as a trend and start embracing it as the foundation of meaningful storytelling.

Hollywood wields immense cultural power, and with that comes great responsibility (Excuse the Spiderman reference). As consumers of media, we must remain vigilant and critical, questioning the narratives presented to us on screen. Only by recognizing and challenging the industry's role in spreading propaganda and ignorance can we hope to see a more honest, diverse, and enlightening cinematic landscape in the future.

Chapter 6

THE WAR ON EXPERTISE

To reject the advice of experts
is to assert autonomy… - Thomas M. Nichols

There was a time when expertise commanded respect. Professionals spent years honing their craft, and their knowledge was valued precisely because it was hard-earned. But in the age of social media and limitless online information, that dynamic has shifted. The phrase "Do your own research" has become a rallying cry, not for genuine inquiry, but often as a way to dismiss expert consensus in favor of personal opinion.

While critical thinking is important, it becomes dangerous when it fuels outright rejection of credible expertise. We've seen it play out repeatedly. Medical professionals spend decades studying epidemiology, yet their advice is brushed aside in favor of alternative treatments promoted by social media influencers with no qualifications beyond a camera and confidence.

YouTube influencers have gained significant influence, sometimes rivaling or surpassing traditional experts in terms of public trust. A study found that 4 in 10 YouTube subscribers aged 18-34 believe their favourite creator understands them better than their friends. This highlights the power of perceived authenticity and relatability in the digital age.

However, it's crucial to distinguish between different types of influencers and their credibility. Key Opinion Leaders (KOLs) often have genuine expertise in their fields, while social media influencers may primarily rely on their large followings and content creation skills. For example, Gordon Ramsay is both a respected chef (KOL) and a social media influencer, combining professional expertise with online reach.

It's important to note that expertise and lived experience are not mutually exclusive. In fact, personal experiences can provide valuable insights, particularly on topics such as religion, racism, bigotry, and trauma. These lived experiences can complement and enrich academic or professional expertise, offering a more comprehensive understanding of complex issues. For instance, someone who has experienced racial discrimination firsthand may offer invaluable perspectives that complement the work of sociologists studying systemic racism. Similarly, individuals who have survived trauma may provide insights that enhance the understanding of mental health professionals.

Moreover, it's worth recognizing that thorough, well-conducted research by non-experts can also contribute to knowledge. Citizen scientists, investigative journalists, and dedicated hobbyists have made significant contributions to various fields. The key is to approach such research critically, verifying sources and methodologies.

The Rise of Scepticism Toward Experts

The erosion of trust in experts is driven by several factors, including scandals, misinformation, and political polarization. High-profile failures, such as the 2008 financial crisis, have led to widespread scepticism about the competence and motives of experts. The global economic collapse, which was facilitated by financial institutions and experts in banking, resulted in massive public disillusionment. This failure allowed populist movements to argue that experts were not only incompetent but also complicit in maintaining a corrupt system.

The Theranos scandal represents a striking failure of both technical and financial expertise. Elizabeth Holmes managed to convince numerous highly respected experts, including medical professionals, venture capitalists, and distinguished board members, that her blood-testing technology was revolutionary. Major investors and media outlets accepted and promoted these claims based on expert endorsements. When the technology was revealed to be fraudulent in 2015, it highlighted how even sophisticated experts could be thoroughly deceived, damaging public trust in both medical and investment expertise.

The Boeing 737 MAX crisis of 2018-2019 serves as another powerful example. Aviation safety experts and regulators at the FAA, long considered the global gold standard in aircraft certification, approved the aircraft despite its fundamental design flaws. The subsequent crashes and revelations about the certification process showed how corporate pressure could compromise expert judgement even in matters of life and death.

This case was particularly damaging to public trust

because aviation safety had long been considered a sphere where expert oversight was uniquely reliable and rigorous.

At the same time, the internet has democratized information but also undermined authority, as anyone with an opinion can present themselves as an expert. This phenomenon has been amplified by social media platforms, where individuals without formal training or knowledge can gain significant influence simply by being charismatic or provocative.

The Democratization of Knowledge

This democratization of knowledge is, in many ways, a double-edged sword. It has empowered individuals to question authority and think critically, but it has also created the illusion that all knowledge is equal. The result is an epidemic of overconfidence, which psychologist David Dunning (of the Dunning-Kruger effect) calls "illusory superiority." In short, people with little knowledge often overestimate their understanding, while experts who are aware of the complexities of their fields, tend to underestimate theirs.

This dynamic has been dramatically amplified by the internet and social media platforms, where complex topics are often reduced to easily digestible sound bites and oversimplified explanations. Someone who reads a few articles about vaccines, for instance, might feel qualified to challenge the conclusions of immunologists who have spent decades in the field. This false equivalence between superficial knowledge and deep expertise has been particularly evident in debates about climate change, where individuals who have read a handful of contrarian blog posts feel confident disputing the consensus of climate scientists. The problem is compounded by the way modern media platforms reward certainty over nuance.

Experts who acknowledge the limitations and uncertainties in their field often appear less convincing to the public than confident amateurs who speak in absolutes. This creates a perverse incentive structure where nuanced, scientifically accurate information is disadvantaged in the marketplace of ideas.

The Death of Expertise

In his book The Death of Expertise, Tom Nichols describes the cultural shift that has eroded trust in professionals. Nichols argues that many people no longer view expertise as a product of rigorous study and experience but as an elitist construct designed to oppress the "common person."

This transformation reflects a broader cultural shift in how knowledge and authority are perceived. The traditional pathways to expertise, which is years of study, apprenticeship, peer review, and professional certification, are increasingly viewed with suspicion rather than respect. This skepticism has been fueled by a populist narrative that frames experts as out-of-touch elites who are disconnected from the real-world experiences of ordinary people.

The democratization of information through the internet has accelerated this trend by creating what Nichols calls the "Google-fueled, Wikipedia-based, blog-sodden" collapse of any division between professionals and laypeople. When anyone can access vast amounts of information instantly, the years spent developing deep expertise can seem unnecessary or even wasteful. This has led to what he terms "the death of expertise." This is not just disagreement with experts but an active rejection of the very idea that specialized knowledge should carry more weight than personal opinion.

This shift has profound implications for public discourse and policy-making. In fields ranging from climate science to public health, expert recommendations are increasingly viewed through a political rather than scientific lens. The rejection of expertise has become intertwined with identity politics, where dismissing expert opinion is seen as an act of resistance against perceived elite dominance.

Nichols points out that this phenomenon is particularly dangerous because it coincides with increasingly complex global challenges that require sophisticated technical solutions. Climate change, pandemic response, artificial intelligence regulation, and other critical issues cannot be effectively addressed without relying on deep technical expertise. Yet at precisely the moment when expert knowledge is most crucial, public trust in expertise is at a historic low.

The situation is exacerbated by what Nichols calls the "cult of conversation," where every issue, no matter how technical, must be debated as if all opinions carry equal weight. This has created a paradoxical situation where experts are expected to "debate" their findings with non-experts as equals, while simultaneously being criticized for appearing condescending when they attempt to explain complex concepts to laypeople.

The financial incentives of modern media have also contributed to this problem. News organizations and social media platforms often present expert opinions alongside non-expert views in the name of "balance," creating a false equivalence that further erodes the authority of genuine expertise. This has created what Nichols describes as a "marketplace of ideas" where the most entertaining or provocative views often triumph over the most accurate or well-researched ones.

The consequences of this shift extend beyond academic debates into practical policy-making and public safety. When large segments of the population reject expert guidance on issues like vaccination or climate change, it becomes increasingly difficult to implement evidence-based solutions to critical problems. This creates a dangerous feedback loop where the rejection of expertise leads to policy failures, which in turn further erodes trust in institutions and experts.

Nichols argues that rebuilding trust in expertise requires addressing both the supply and demand sides of the problem. Experts need to become better communicators and more transparent about their methods and limitations. At the same time, the public needs to develop better critical thinking skills and a more nuanced understanding of how expert knowledge is developed and validated. This includes recognizing that questioning experts is healthy, but wholesale rejection of expertise is dangerous. The challenge moving forward is to find ways to restore the value of expertise while acknowledging legitimate critiques of how expert authority has sometimes been misused.

This requires building new models of engagement between experts and the public that maintain rigorous standards while being more inclusive and transparent.

The Consequences of Ignoring Expertise

Perhaps the most concerning is the long-term impact on scientific research and professional expertise itself. When society consistently devalues expert knowledge, it creates disincentives for pursuing deep expertise in any field. Why spend years mastering a complex subject if that knowledge will be given no more weight than a casual opinion? This dynamic threatens to create a feedback loop where the quality of available expertise gradually diminishes, further reinforcing public scepticism.

The rejection of expertise also has serious implications for democracy. While democratic societies rightly emphasize the importance of public participation in decision-making, effective governance requires balancing popular opinion with expert knowledge. When expertise is systematically dismissed, it becomes increasingly difficult to implement evidence-based policies or address complex challenges that require technical understanding. This can lead to what some political scientists call "policy paralysis" – a situation where necessary but technically complex solutions cannot be implemented due to public resistance based on misunderstanding or mistrust.

The economic consequences of expertise rejection are equally concerning. In an increasingly complex global economy, competitive advantage often depends on leveraging specialized knowledge and technical innovation. Countries or regions that systematically dismiss expertise risk falling behind in economic development, scientific advancement, and technological innovation. This has implications not just for economic growth but for national security and global influence as well.

Moreover, the rejection of expertise often hits vulnerable populations hardest. When public health expertise is ignored, it's often disadvantaged communities that suffer the worst consequences. When environmental regulations are dismissed, it's typically lower-income neighbourhoods that bear the brunt of pollution and environmental degradation.

When financial expertise is disregarded, it's usually ordinary investors and consumers who pay the price while the well-informed and wealthy protect themselves.

Erosion of Institutions

The systematic erosion of trust in institutions represents one of the most significant challenges facing modern society. As experts face increasing skepticism and outright hostility, the institutions they represent, from universities and research centers to public health agencies and regulatory bodies, have seen their authority and credibility steadily decline. This deterioration of institutional trust threatens not just these organizations themselves, but the very foundations of societal progress and collective action.

The consequences of this institutional erosion are far-reaching and profound. When citizens lose faith in the Centers for Disease Control's recommendations, or dismiss the findings of climate scientists at prestigious research institutions, our ability to address complex challenges becomes severely compromised. The power of institutions lies not just in their accumulated expertise, but in their capacity to coordinate responses to societal challenges and maintain stable frameworks for progress.

Consider the role of educational institutions. Universities have traditionally served as centres of knowledge creation and validation, places where ideas are tested, refined, and transmitted to new generations. When their authority is undermined, the very process of knowledge creation becomes suspect. We see this playing out in current debates over curriculum content, research funding, and academic freedom. The questioning of institutional expertise has led to situations where established scientific principles are treated as mere opinions, and rigorous research findings are dismissed if they conflict with political or ideological preferences.

This erosion of institutional authority creates a dangerous vacuum. Nature abhors a vacuum, and in the absence of trusted institutional voices, alternative sources of authority emerge. Social media influencers, political pundits, and self-proclaimed experts rush to fill the void, often promoting simplified or distorted versions of complex issues. Unlike traditional institutions, these new authority figures often lack accountability mechanisms, peer review processes, or the institutional memory that helps prevent repeated mistakes.

The impact on public health institutions provides a particularly stark example. When epidemics and pandemics strike, many public health agencies find their recommendations questioned or ignored, not because of scientific inadequacy, but because institutional authority had already been severely eroded. The consequences are measured not just in policy failures but in lives lost. This same pattern threatens our ability to address future public health challenges, from emerging infectious diseases to the health impacts of climate change.

Scientific research institutions face similar challenges. The politicization of climate science illustrates how the erosion of institutional authority can paralyze society's response to existential threats. When research institutions are viewed not as sources of objective knowledge but as political actors with agendas, their ability to inform public policy becomes severely compromised. This dynamic creates a dangerous feedback loop: as institutional recommendations are ignored, problems worsen, further undermining public trust in institutional expertise.

The judiciary and legal institutions face similar challenges. When courts and legal experts are viewed as political actors rather than arbiters of justice, the very foundation of the rule of law becomes unstable. This erosion of trust in legal institutions threatens not just the administration of justice but the basic social contract that enables complex societies to function.

So what are the broader implications of this institutional erosion?

First, it threatens our ability to achieve consensus on basic facts, making policy debates increasingly disconnected from reality. When institutional expertise is dismissed, debates become exercises in rhetoric rather than evidence-based discussions of solutions.

Second, it compromises our ability to address long-term challenges. Institutions serve as repositories of knowledge and experience, maintaining continuity across political cycles and generational changes. When their authority erodes, society loses this long-term perspective, becoming more susceptible to short-term thinking and quick-fix solutions.

Third, it undermines the development of future expertise. Young people observing the public dismissal of institutional expertise may question the value of pursuing advanced education or specialized knowledge. This threatens the pipeline of future experts needed to address tomorrow's challenges.

Fourth, it weakens social cohesion. Institutions serve as shared reference points in society, places where different perspectives can be evaluated against common standards of evidence and logic. When these shared reference points disappear, society fragments into competing reality bubbles, making collective action increasingly difficult.

The path to rebuilding institutional trust will not be easy, but several steps are essential.

First, institutions themselves must adapt to changing social conditions without compromising their core functions. This means becoming more transparent in their processes, more inclusive in their perspectives, and more effective in communicating their findings to the public.

Second, education systems need to place greater emphasis on understanding how institutions function and why they matter. This includes teaching about the processes of peer review, the importance of institutional memory, and the role of specialized expertise in addressing complex challenges.

Third, new mechanisms for institutional accountability need to be developed that maintain rigour while addressing legitimate public concerns about institutional bias or capture by special interests. This might include new forms of public oversight, improved transparency measures, or innovative approaches to stakeholder engagement.

Fourth, media literacy programs need to be strengthened to help citizens better understand the difference between institutional expertise and unsubstantiated opinion. This includes developing better tools for evaluating sources of information and understanding the processes behind institutional knowledge creation.

The stakes in this struggle are enormous. Institutions serve as the immune system of society, helping to identify and address challenges before they become crises. When this immune system is compromised, society becomes more vulnerable to a range of threats, from pandemic diseases to economic instability to environmental degradation.

Moreover, institutions play a crucial role in maintaining the complex systems that support modern civilization. From electrical grids to food safety systems to financial networks, our daily lives depend on institutional expertise functioning effectively. The erosion of institutional authority threatens not just abstract principles but the practical foundations of modern society.

The way forward requires finding a balance between legitimate critique of institutions and wholesale rejection of institutional authority. Institutions must be able to evolve and improve while maintaining their essential functions. This means creating new frameworks for institutional accountability that strengthen rather than undermine institutional authority.

Success in this endeavour is crucial for addressing the complex challenges facing modern society. Climate change, technological disruption, demographic shifts, and other major challenges require coordinated responses based on institutional expertise. Without trusted institutions to guide these responses, our ability to navigate these challenges is severely compromised.

The erosion of institutional authority represents a crisis that threatens the foundations of social progress. Addressing this crisis requires not just defending institutions but re-imagining how they can function in an age of widespread scepticism and rapid social change. Our future depends on finding ways to rebuild trust in the institutions that make collective action and social progress possible.

Finally, it is crucial to foster intellectual humility, both in experts and the general public. Experts must acknowledge the limits of their knowledge and avoid the appearance of arrogance, while the public must recognize that expertise, while imperfect, is vital for navigating the complexities of the modern world.

The war on expertise is not a battle society can afford to lose. Without trust in professionals and institutions, we risk descending into a state of chaos where facts are malleable, and ignorance reigns supreme.

Chapter 7

The Cult of Conspiracy Theories

Conspiracy is a small but durable seller,
retooled every year or so. - John Gregory Dunne

Conspiracy theories have always been a part of human history, but their prevalence and impact have grown significantly in the modern era. From QAnon and Flat Earth theories to anti-vaccine movements and the belief that the moon landing was staged, the rise of conspiracy thinking has become a defining feature of modern discourse. But conspiracy theories are not just harmless speculation; they have real-world consequences, influencing elections, public health policies, and even acts of violence.

What is it about conspiracy theories that makes them so alluring? Why do so many people reject expert analysis in favour of elaborate, often baseless, alternative narratives? And more importantly, how can societies combat the spread of dangerous misinformation while respecting free thought and scepticism?

The Psychology of Conspiracy Thinking

When faced with uncertainty, chaos, or complex global events, humans naturally seek explanations that can make sense of their world. Conspiracy theories, with their neat narratives and clear villains, offer seemingly simple answers to complicated questions. At their core, conspiracy theories appeal to fundamental psychological needs: the need for certainty, control, and belonging. Understanding this psychological foundation is crucial for addressing the growing influence of conspiracy thinking in our modern society.

The appeal of conspiracy theories lies not in their factual basis but in their emotional resonance. When people feel powerless or uncertain, conspiracy theories provide a framework that explains their experiences and identifies clear sources of blame. Whether it's attributing global events to secret cabals or claiming that powerful institutions are hiding "the truth," these theories transform the messy complexity of reality into straightforward narratives of good versus evil.

The need for certainty drives much of conspiracy thinking. In a world of increasing complexity, where experts often qualify their statements and acknowledge uncertainty, conspiracy theories offer the comfort of absolute answers. They replace probabilistic thinking and nuanced analysis with definitive explanations. This certainty is particularly appealing during times of crisis or rapid social change, when traditional sources of authority seem unable to provide clear answers or effective solutions.

The psychological appeal of control also plays a crucial role. Conspiracy theories suggest that events are not random but carefully orchestrated by powerful actors. Paradoxically, many people find this idea more comforting than accepting that major events might result from chance, incompetence, or complex systemic factors. The belief that someone is "pulling the strings" implies that someone is in control, even if that control is malevolent. This can feel preferable to accepting that sometimes terrible things happen without any grand plan or purpose.

The need for belonging drives the social aspect of conspiracy belief. Conspiracy communities provide their members with a sense of special knowledge and shared understanding. Being "in the know" about supposed hidden truths creates a powerful in-group identity. Members of these communities often view themselves as "awakened" individuals who see through the deceptions that fool the general public. This sense of special insight can be incredibly appealing, particularly for people who feel marginalized or disconnected from mainstream society.

Modern technology and social media have amplified these psychological dynamics. Online platforms create echo chambers where conspiracy beliefs can flourish unchallenged. The algorithms that drive these platforms often promote engaging content over accurate content, and conspiracy theories, with their emotional appeal and dramatic narratives, tend to generate high engagement. This creates a self-reinforcing cycle where exposure to conspiracy content leads to more conspiracy content, gradually shifting people's perception of what constitutes reliable information.

The role of social identity in conspiracy thinking cannot be overstated. Once conspiracy beliefs become part of someone's identity, challenging these beliefs can feel like a personal attack. This explains why presenting facts or evidence that contradict conspiracy theories often fails to change minds and may even strengthen existing beliefs. When faced with contradictory evidence, believers often engage in motivated reasoning, finding ways to discount or reinterpret information that challenges their beliefs.

The impact of conspiracy thinking extends far beyond individual psychology. When significant portions of society embrace conspiracy theories, it becomes increasingly difficult to achieve consensus on basic facts or implement evidence-based solutions to real problems. This has serious implications for public health, democratic governance, and social cohesion. The COVID-19 pandemic provided numerous examples of how conspiracy beliefs about vaccines, mask-wearing, and public health measures complicated efforts to control the virus's spread.

Education level and critical thinking skills, while important, do not provide complete immunity to conspiracy thinking. Highly educated individuals can be susceptible to conspiracy beliefs, particularly in areas outside their expertise. This suggests that the appeal of conspiracy theories isn't simply about lack of knowledge or intelligence, but rather about deeper psychological and emotional needs that these theories fulfill.

The internet age has created perfect conditions for conspiracy theories to flourish. The democratization of information, while valuable in many ways, has also made it easier for conspiracy theories to spread and harder for people to distinguish between reliable and unreliable sources. The decline of traditional gatekeepers of information, combined with the rise of alternative media platforms, has created an environment where conspiracy theories can quickly reach large audiences.

The relationship between conspiracy thinking and

political polarization is particularly concerning. When conspiracy theories become aligned with political identities, they become even more resistant to correction. Political actors may exploit and encourage conspiracy thinking for their own purposes, further entrenching these beliefs and making them part of broader ideological frameworks.

The challenge of addressing conspiracy thinking is complicated by the fact that not all conspiracy theories are false. History provides examples of real conspiracies that were eventually exposed. This reality makes it harder to dismiss conspiracy theories outright and provides believers with ready examples to justify their scepticism of official narratives. The key is developing the critical thinking skills to distinguish between reasonable scepticism and unfounded conspiracy beliefs.

The path forward requires understanding and addressing the psychological needs that make conspiracy theories appealing. Simply dismissing conspiracy believers as irrational or uninformed is unlikely to be effective and may reinforce their beliefs. Instead, we need approaches that acknowledge the legitimate concerns and emotions that drive conspiracy thinking while helping people develop more constructive ways to address these needs.

Building resilience against conspiracy thinking requires several approaches. Education should focus not just on facts but on understanding how knowledge is created and validated. This includes teaching about the scientific method, the importance of evidence, and the difference between correlation and causation. People need tools to evaluate claims and understand why certain sources of information are more reliable than others.

We need to address the social and emotional needs that make conspiracy theories appealing. This might include creating alternative communities and sources of meaning, helping people develop a sense of agency and control in their lives, and providing ways to engage with complex issues that don't require embracing conspiracy theories.

Media literacy education needs to be updated for the digital age. People need to understand how social media algorithms work, how misinformation spreads, and how to evaluate online sources of information. This includes recognizing the signs of conspiracy thinking and understanding the psychological tactics that conspiracy theories often employ.

In addition we need to improve how legitimate institutions communicate with the public. When official sources appear distant, untrustworthy, or unable to provide clear answers, it creates space for conspiracy theories to flourish. Institutions need to find ways to maintain scientific rigour while communicating more effectively with the public.

The psychology of conspiracy thinking reminds us that human beings are not purely rational actors. We are emotional and social creatures, seeking meaning and connection in a complex world. Understanding this aspect of human nature is crucial for addressing the challenge of conspiracy thinking in modern society.

As we move forward, the goal should not be to eliminate all scepticism or questioning of official narratives. Rather, we need to foster healthy scepticism that is grounded in evidence and critical thinking rather than in psychological needs and emotional appeals. This requires creating social and institutional frameworks that help people meet their needs for certainty, control, and belonging in more constructive ways.

The prevalence of conspiracy thinking in modern society represents both a symptom of deeper social issues and a challenge that needs to be addressed. By understanding the psychology behind conspiracy beliefs, we can develop more effective approaches to building a society that is both critically minded and resistant to unfounded conspiracy theories. This is crucial not just for individual well-being but for the health of our democratic institutions and our ability to address real challenges facing society.

Historical Context: Conspiracy Theories Through the Ages

Conspiracy theories are not a modern invention; they have deep historical roots. Ancient myths often attributed natural disasters or societal changes to the actions of gods or secretive groups. In more recent history, the Protocols of the Elders of Zion, a fabricated text claiming a Jewish conspiracy for world domination, fueled anti-Semitism and influenced political movements in the early 20th century. Similarly, the assassination of President John F. Kennedy spawned countless conspiracy theories, reflecting public distrust of official narratives.

These historical examples illustrate the enduring appeal of conspiracy theories and their ability to shape societies and political movements. Understanding this context is crucial to addressing the modern resurgence of conspiracy thinking.

Conspiracy Theories in Action

David Icke: The Pied Piper of Conspiracy Theories

In the vast landscape of conspiracy theories, few figures loom as large as David Icke. A former footballer and sports broadcaster turned self-proclaimed "son of God," Icke has spent decades weaving an intricate tapestry of alternative narratives that challenge conventional wisdom and established power structures.

As someone who has read some of Icke's books during the early stages of my own journey away from organized religion, I can attest to the allure of his ideas. His work offers a grand, unified theory of everything, connecting disparate events and phenomena into a cohesive narrative that promises to explain the hidden machinations of our world.

Icke's theories are as diverse as they are controversial. From his claims of reptilian shape-shifters controlling world governments to his assertions about the illusory nature of reality, Icke has never shied away from ideas that most would consider outlandish. His work on the "Babylonian Brotherhood" and the "Global Elite" has resonated with those who feel disenfranchised by traditional power structures.

However, it's crucial to approach Icke's ideas with a critical eye. While his work has undoubtedly contributed to the popularization of conspiracy theories, it has also been criticized for promoting harmful misinformation. His recent claims linking 5G technology to the COVID-19 pandemic, for instance, have been widely debunked and led to his de-platforming from major social media sites.

Icke's influence extends far beyond his books and lectures. He has become a lightning rod for controversy, with his ideas finding new life in the digital age. The COVID-19 pandemic, in particular, has seen a resurgence of interest in Icke's theories, as people search for explanations in uncertain times.

Yet, it's important to recognize the potential dangers of uncritically accepting conspiracy theories. While questioning authority and seeking alternative explanations can be healthy, wholesale adoption of unsubstantiated claims can lead to real-world harm. The arson attacks on 5G towers following Icke's claims serve as a stark reminder of this reality.

Despite the controversies, Icke's enduring popularity speaks to a deeper societal need. In a world of increasing complexity and uncertainty, his theories offer simple explanations and a sense of control. They provide a narrative that makes sense of chaos, even if that narrative is ultimately flawed.

As we navigate the information age, it's crucial to strike a balance between open-mindedness and critical thinking. While figures like Icke challenge us to question our assumptions, we must also be willing to subject their claims to rigorous scrutiny.

The Rise of QAnon

What began as cryptic posts on an obscure internet forum has evolved into one of the most significant conspiracy movements in modern history. QAnon's core narrative, alleging a global cabal of Satan-worshipping paedophiles controlling governments and media, might seem too fantastic for widespread belief. Yet this conspiracy theory has attracted millions of followers worldwide and influenced political discourse at the highest levels.

The movement's growth reveals how modern conspiracy theories can adapt and evolve to incorporate new events and attract diverse adherents. QAnon has absorbed other conspiracy theories, from anti-vaccine sentiment to election fraud claims, creating a grand unified theory of conspiracy that offers believers an all-encompassing worldview. This flexibility has helped it survive repeated failed predictions and maintain its appeal even after its anonymous prophet "Q" ceased posting.

The movement's impact reached its apex during the January 6, 2021, Capitol riot, where QAnon followers were prominently represented among insurrectionists.

This event demonstrated how online conspiracy theories can motivate real-world violence and threaten democratic institutions. The presence of QAnon believers in elected offices and their influence on political discourse continues to pose challenges for democratic governance and social stability.

The Anti-Vaccine Movement

The modern anti-vaccine movement represents one of the most direct threats to public health emerging from conspiracy thinking. While vaccine hesitancy has existed since the first vaccines were developed, social media has allowed anti-vaccine conspiracy theories to reach unprecedented audiences and achieve new levels of sophistication.

The movement's core claims, that vaccines cause autism, contain dangerous toxins, or represent a profit-driven conspiracy by pharmaceutical companies, have been thoroughly debunked by scientific research. Yet these ideas persist and evolve, affecting global health initiatives.

The origins of today's anti-vaccine movement can be traced to a now-thoroughly discredited 1998 study by Andrew Wakefield that suggested a link between the MMR vaccine and autism. Though the study was based on just 12 children and was later revealed to be fraudulent, leading to Wakefield losing his medical license, the damage was done. The study sparked a fear that continues to resonate with parents and has been amplified by social media, celebrity endorsements, and a growing distrust in medical institutions.

What makes this movement particularly fascinating and troubling is its demographic make-up. Unlike many other conspiracy movements, anti-vaccine sentiment often finds its strongest support among well-educated, affluent parents. These are individuals who have the resources and capability to research health decisions for their children, yet often fall prey to misinformation and pseudo-scientific claims. This paradox highlights how even intelligent, well-meaning people can be led astray when emotional fears override rational analysis.

The movement's evolution in recent years has been particularly concerning. What began as specific concerns about the MMR vaccine has morphed into a broader ideology that questions all vaccines and the entire concept of vaccination. Modern anti-vaccine activists have created a sophisticated ecosystem of alternative media, advocacy organizations, and political action groups. They've also become adept at using social media to spread their message, often employing emotional narratives and personal anecdotes that resonate more powerfully than statistical evidence or scientific studies.

The consequences of this movement are both concrete and tragic. We've seen the resurgence of previously controlled diseases like measles in communities with low vaccination rates. During the COVID-19 pandemic, anti-vaccine sentiment contributed to unnecessary deaths and prolonged the public health crisis. The movement has also damaged public trust in other medical interventions and public health initiatives, creating ripple effects that extend far beyond vaccination.

Perhaps most troubling is how the movement has

undermined the relationship between patients and healthcare providers. Doctors report spending increasing amounts of time countering vaccine misinformation, often with limited success. The movement has created an alternative universe of health information that makes it difficult for medical professionals to establish the trust necessary for effective healthcare delivery.

The success of the anti-vaccine movement also reveals deeper problems in our society. It highlights the growing distrust in traditional sources of authority and expertise, the challenges of communicating scientific information to the public, and the power of social media to spread misinformation. These are issues that extend far beyond vaccination and threaten our ability to address other complex challenges facing society.

The movement's rhetoric often focuses on "medical freedom" and "parental choice," framing vaccination as a personal decision rather than a public health issue. This framing ignores the communal nature of infectious disease prevention and the concept of herd immunity. When individuals choose not to vaccinate, they put not only themselves at risk but also those who cannot be vaccinated due to age or medical conditions.

The financial aspects of the anti-vaccine movement deserve particular scrutiny. While activists often accuse pharmaceutical companies of profiting from vaccines (ignoring that vaccines represent a tiny fraction of pharmaceutical profits), the movement itself has developed its own profitable ecosystem. Alternative health products, books, documentaries, and speaking engagements generate significant revenue for prominent anti-vaccine advocates. This creates a financial incentive to perpetuate vaccine fears and resist scientific evidence that might threaten this business model.

The movement's success in political advocacy is

equally concerning. Anti-vaccine activists have successfully lobbied for expanded vaccine exemptions in many states in the U.S. and have gained supporters in state legislatures and Congress. This political influence threatens to undermine public health policies that have protected communities for generations.

Addressing the challenge of vaccine resistance requires a multi-faceted approach. Simply presenting scientific evidence isn't enough, as many anti-vaccine believers are impervious to contradictory information once they've adopted these beliefs. Instead, we need strategies that address the psychological and social factors that make anti-vaccine messages appealing.

The persistence of anti-vaccine beliefs despite overwhelming scientific evidence illustrates how conspiracy theories can override rational decision-making when they tap into deep-seated fears and distrust of institutions. The movement has been particularly successful in using social media to spread emotional narratives and misrepresented scientific information, creating doubt even among those who might otherwise accept scientific consensus.

Climate Change Denial

Climate change denial represents one of the most consequential and well-funded conspiracy movements in history. Unlike many conspiracy theories that emerge organically from grassroots misconceptions, climate change denial has been deliberately cultivated and sustained through a sophisticated network of industry-funded think tanks, pseudo-experts, and media campaigns. This orchestrated effort to undermine climate science has delayed crucial action on global warming for decades, with potentially catastrophic consequences for our planet.

The roots of modern climate change denial can be traced back to the tobacco industry's playbook of manufacturing doubt about scientific evidence. Many of the same organizations and individuals who worked to question the link between smoking and cancer later turned their attention to climate science. Their strategy wasn't to prove climate change wrong—they knew they couldn't—but rather to create enough doubt to paralyze policy action.

The conspiracy theories surrounding climate change have evolved over time, adapting as the evidence for global warming has become increasingly undeniable. The movement began with outright denial of temperature rises, then shifted to questioning human responsibility, and now often focuses on downplaying the risks or arguing that proposed solutions are part of a sinister agenda. This evolution reveals the true nature of climate denial: it's not about scientific truth but about protecting vested interests.

The core conspiracy theories promoted by climate change deniers typically fall into several categories.

First, there's the "hoax" narrative, which suggests that thousands of scientists worldwide are fabricating evidence of climate change to secure research funding or advance a political agenda. This theory requires believing that scientists from different countries, cultures, and political systems have maintained a perfect conspiracy for decades without a single credible whistle-blower emerging.

Then, there's the "natural cycles" argument, which acknowledges warming but denies human responsibility. While this seems more reasonable on the surface, it ignores the vast body of evidence showing how human activities have accelerated warming far beyond natural variations. This theory often involves cherry-picking data and misrepresenting historical climate patterns.

Additionally, there's the "great reset" conspiracy, which frames climate action as a plot by global elites to control the economy and restrict individual freedoms. This narrative has gained particular traction in recent years, merging with other conspiracy theories about world governance and economic control.

The success of these conspiracy theories relies heavily on exploiting legitimate concerns about economic change and government overreach. Climate denial movements have been particularly effective at linking environmental regulations to fears about job losses and economic decline in fossil fuel-dependent communities. This creates a powerful emotional barrier to accepting climate science, as it requires confronting difficult truths about the need for economic transformation.

The financial backing behind climate denial reveals its true nature as a coordinated disinformation campaign rather than a genuine scientific debate. Investigations have revealed how fossil fuel companies spent millions funding organizations that promote climate denial, while internally acknowledging the reality of climate change. This duplicity exposes the cynical nature of climate denial conspiracy theories. They are tools designed to protect profits rather than pursue truth.

Social media has amplified these conspiracy theories, creating echo chambers where climate denial can flourish unchallenged. The algorithms that drive these platforms often promote controversial content over scientific consensus, making it easier for people to find and share climate denial content than to access accurate climate science information.

The consequences of climate denial extend far

beyond the realm of scientific debate. By delaying action on climate change, these conspiracy theories have contributed to a situation where more drastic measures will now be needed to address global warming. The time lost to manufactured doubt has made the challenge of transitioning to a sustainable economy more difficult and costly.

Particularly troubling is how climate denial has become intertwined with political identity in many countries. When belief or disbelief in climate science becomes a marker of political allegiance, it becomes incredibly difficult to have rational discussions about climate policy. This politicization of science represents one of the most damaging effects of climate denial conspiracy theories.

The movement has also undermined public trust in scientific institutions more broadly. By portraying climate scientists as corrupt or politically motivated, climate denial has contributed to a broader scepticism of scientific expertise. This erosion of trust has implications far beyond climate science, affecting public response to other scientific issues from vaccination to public health measures.

The psychological appeal of climate denial conspiracy theories is important to understand. They offer simple villains (corrupt scientists, power-hungry politicians) instead of complex systemic problems. They provide the comfort of believing that no major changes to our lifestyle or economy are necessary. They allow people to avoid the anxiety and guilt that might come with acknowledging our role in climate change.

The Role of Storytelling and Narrative

Conspiracy theories are often compelling because they use powerful narratives to attract followers. These narratives typically feature clear heroes and villains, dramatic plots, and a sense of urgency. To counter conspiracy theories, it is essential to offer equally compelling, evidence-based stories that resonate with individuals' values and beliefs.

For example, public health campaigns that emphasize community and shared responsibility can counter anti-vaccine narratives. Similarly, climate change communication that highlights local impacts and solutions can address scepticism and denial. By harnessing the power of storytelling, we can challenge conspiracy theories and promote evidence-based reasoning.

The cult of conspiracy theories is a significant challenge in the modern era, fueled by psychological, social, and technological factors. By understanding the mechanisms behind conspiracy thinking, we can begin to address its root causes and mitigate its impact.

This requires a multifaceted approach that combines education, critical thinking, and effective communication. Only by confronting conspiracy theories head-on can we hope to build a society that values truth, evidence, and rational thought.

Chapter 8

Education: A Double-Edged Sword

If you think education is expensive, try ignorance.
- Jeff Rich

Education is indeed often heralded as the great equalizer, the cornerstone of progress and enlightenment. Its potential to transform lives and societies is immense, offering individuals the tools to understand the world around them, think critically, and pursue their aspirations. At its best, education can challenge ignorance, dismantle prejudice, and inspire innovation, serving as a catalyst for personal growth and societal advancement.

The power of education to challenge ignorance is evident in how it exposes individuals to diverse ideas, cultures, and perspectives. By broadening horizons and encouraging critical thinking, education can help break down stereotypes and foster empathy. For instance, comprehensive sex education has been shown to reduce teen pregnancy rates and promote healthier relationships, demonstrating how knowledge can directly combat ignorance and its consequences.

Education's role in dismantling prejudice is closely linked to its ability to challenge ignorance. By providing accurate information about different groups of people, their histories, and contributions to society, education can help erode the foundations of discrimination. The inclusion of diverse voices and narratives in curricula can help students develop a more nuanced understanding of the world, fostering tolerance and respect for differences.

Moreover, education is a key driver of innovation. By equipping individuals with knowledge and skills, it empowers them to solve problems creatively and push the boundaries of human understanding. The rapid advancements in fields like technology, medicine, and environmental science are testament to the power of education to drive progress.

The Ideal: Education as a Path to Enlightenment

At its best, education instils a thirst for knowledge, the ability to think critically, and an openness to new ideas. It encourages individuals to question the status quo, seek evidence, and make informed decisions. Historically, some of humanity's greatest achievements, such as medical breakthroughs, technological innovations, and social reforms have been built on the foundations of education.

Take, for example, the Enlightenment era. Rooted in education and intellectual inquiry, this period saw the rise of scientific reasoning, the rejection of superstition, and the establishment of modern democracies.

Institutions of higher learning, such as the universities in Bologna, Oxford, and Paris, became incubators of revolutionary thought, birthing ideas that would shape the modern world. However, this ideal vision of education assumes that systems are designed to nurture intellectual growth and that access to education is equitable. Reality often paints a very different picture.

Education as Oppression: The Dark History of Learning as a Weapon of Control

Throughout human history, education has worn two faces: one of liberation and enlightenment, the other of oppression and control. While we often celebrate education's power to empower and elevate, we must also confront its darker legacy as a tool for maintaining social hierarchies and suppressing independent thought. Perhaps nowhere was this more evident than in South Africa's Apartheid education system, which stands as one of the most stark examples of education deliberately designed to restrict rather than expand human potential.

The Apartheid education system, formalized through the Bantu Education Act of 1953, represents the logical extreme of education as oppression. Under this system, Black South Africans were deliberately provided with an inferior education designed to prepare them for lives of servitude. As H.F. Verwoerd, the architect of Apartheid education, chillingly declared, "There is no place for [the African] in the European community above the level of certain forms of labour." The system was explicitly designed to create an underclass, using education not to lift up but to hold down.

This wasn't a bug in the system. It was its primary feature. The Apartheid education system meticulously structured every aspect of learning to reinforce racial hierarchy. Curricula were designed to limit academic ambition, facilities were deliberately under-resourced, and teachers were often underqualified. The goal was not just to provide inferior education but to convince the oppressed of their own inferiority.

But Apartheid education wasn't unique in its fundamental approach. It was merely more honest about its intentions. Throughout history, dominant groups have used education to maintain their power, though usually with more subtle methods. In colonial America, slaves were forbidden from learning to read, while Native American children were forced into residential schools designed to erase their cultural identity. These examples represent the same principle: education as a means of control rather than enlightenment.

Today's educational systems often perpetuate similar patterns of control, albeit in more subtle ways. Standardized testing, while presented as objective measurement, often reinforces existing social hierarchies. Curriculum choices frequently reflect dominant cultural perspectives while marginalizing others. School funding mechanisms, tied to property taxes in many countries, ensure that economic inequality translates directly into educational inequality.

The "hidden curriculum"—the unstated lessons schools teach about authority, compliance, and social hierarchy—continues to shape students in ways that often serve existing power structures. Students learn not just academic subjects but also to accept hierarchy, follow rules without question, and measure their worth through external validation.

Consider how modern schools often emphasize: They stress compliance over creativity, standardized answers over critical thinking, competition over cooperation, conformity over individuality, and authority over autonomy.

These priorities echo the fundamental aims of Apartheid education, though without its explicit racial focus. They serve to create individuals who fit into existing social structures rather than questioning or challenging them. The economic dimension of educational control cannot be ignored. In many countries, access to quality education is increasingly tied to wealth, creating what some scholars call "educational apartheid" based on class rather than race. Student debt serves as a modern form of bondage, ensuring that even those who manage to access higher education often emerge into forms of economic servitude.

The digital age has added new dimensions to educational control. While technology offers unprecedented access to information, it also enables new forms of surveillance, standardization, and behavioural control in educational settings. Online learning platforms can track every interaction, creating detailed profiles of student behaviour and compliance.

However, understanding education's role in social control also illuminates paths for resistance and reform. The same South African students who were subjected to Bantu education became leaders in the fight against Apartheid, turning their understanding of educational oppression into tools for liberation. The Soweto Uprising of 1976, sparked by students protesting the imposition of Afrikaans in schools, demonstrates how awareness of educational oppression can catalyze broader social resistance.

Residential Schools and the Weaponization of Education

One of the most haunting examples of education as a

weapon of cultural destruction can be found in the residential school systems of North America. These institutions, operating under the guise of education, represented a deliberate attempt to erase Indigenous cultures through what amounts to cultural genocide. The motto "Kill the Indian, save the man," coined by Captain Richard H. Pratt, founder of the Carlisle Indian Industrial School, chillingly encapsulates the true purpose of these institutions.

In Canada, the residential school system operated for over a century, with the last school closing in 1996. More than 150,000 First Nations, Inuit, and Métis children were forcibly removed from their families and communities. The statistics are stark, but they fail to capture the full human tragedy: thousands of children died in these institutions, many in unmarked graves that continue to be discovered today. The Truth and Reconciliation Commission of Canada has documented at least 4,100 deaths, though the actual number is likely much higher.

In the United States, the system was equally devastating. Beginning in the 1870s, Native American children were taken from their homes and placed in boarding schools designed to "civilize" them. By 1926, nearly 83% of Native American school-age children were attending these schools. The psychological and cultural damage inflicted by these institutions continues to reverberate through generations.

The methodology of these schools was brutally simple: sever children from their cultural roots and force them to adopt the colonizers' way of life. Upon arrival, children's hair was cut, their traditional clothes were replaced with uniforms, and they were given new, English names. Speaking indigenous languages was strictly forbidden, often under threat of severe physical punishment. The message was clear: their identity was something to be ashamed of, something to be erased.

The curriculum in these schools was designed not to educate but to indoctrinate. Academic instruction was often secondary to manual labor and religious conversion. Girls were taught domestic skills to become servants in white households, while boys were trained in basic agricultural and trade skills. The goal was not to empower these children but to create a subservient underclass, stripped of their cultural identity and prepared for menial roles in colonial society.

The physical and emotional abuse in these institutions was systemic and severe. Children faced punishment for speaking their native languages, practicing traditional spirituality, or even speaking to siblings. Many suffered physical and sexual abuse. Disease was rampant due to poor living conditions, inadequate medical care, and malnutrition. The death rates in some schools reached as high as 60%. But perhaps the most insidious aspect of the residential school system was its attack on family and community bonds. By removing children from their families during their formative years, the system disrupted the transmission of cultural knowledge, parenting skills, and community ties. Many survivors, having been raised without parental models, struggled to raise their own children, creating a cycle of trauma that continues to affect Indigenous communities today.

The legacy of residential schools extends far beyond the immediate survivors. Research has documented inter-generational trauma, with the children and grandchildren of survivors showing higher rates of mental health issues, substance abuse, and suicide. The loss of language and cultural knowledge has left many Indigenous communities struggling to maintain their traditional ways of life.

The damage to Indigenous languages has been particularly severe. Many languages that were once widely spoken are now on the brink of extinction, as the residential school system succeeded in breaking the chain of linguistic transmission between generations. This represents not just the loss of communication tools but the disappearance of unique ways of understanding the world, as Indigenous languages often contain irreplaceable knowledge about local ecosystems, traditional medicines, and cultural practices.

The residential school system also created a profound distrust of educational institutions among many Indigenous people. This legacy continues to affect educational outcomes for Indigenous students today, who often face systemic barriers in accessing quality education while simultaneously dealing with the historical trauma associated with formal schooling.

The recent discoveries of unmarked graves at former residential school sites in Canada have forced a broader reckoning with this dark history. These discoveries have shocked the conscience of many who were unaware of the full extent of the system's brutality. Yet for Indigenous communities, these findings merely confirm what they have known and carried for generations.

The response to these discoveries highlights ongoing tensions in how societies deal with historical injustice. While there have been official apologies and calls for reconciliation, many Indigenous leaders argue that true healing requires more than words. It requires fundamental changes in how educational systems interact with Indigenous communities, recognition of Indigenous sovereignty, and substantial resources for cultural revitalization.

The residential school system represents more than just a historical tragedy; it serves as a warning about how educational institutions can be weaponized for cultural destruction. This history raises crucial questions about current educational practices and policies, particularly regarding minority and Indigenous communities.

Today, as we witness attempts to restrict teaching about racial history in various jurisdictions, the lessons of the residential school system become particularly relevant. The impulse to use education to suppress certain narratives or identities continues, albeit in different forms.

Colonial Education Systems:

In colonized regions, education was often weaponized to erase indigenous cultures and impose the values of the colonizers. Residential schools in Canada and the United States, for instance, aimed to assimilate indigenous children by suppressing their languages, traditions, and identities.

Censorship in Curriculum:

The relationship between state power and education has always been complex, but perhaps nowhere is this more evident than in the deliberate manipulation of historical narratives in educational systems. When governments assert control over what students learn about their nation's past, they don't just edit textbooks – they reshape collective memory and national identity for generations to come. State control over education operates through multiple mechanisms, each more subtle than the last.

The most obvious is direct censorship: the removal of controversial events, figures, or movements from textbooks and curricula. But the more insidious methods involve careful framing, selective emphasis, and the creation of particular emotional associations with historical events.

Consider how authoritarian regimes typically handle their revolutionary origins. Rather than presenting the complex web of social, economic, and political factors that led to change, they often reduce history to a simplistic narrative of heroic struggle against clearly defined villains. Nuance disappears, replaced by a mythology that serves current power structures.

The impact extends far beyond just historical knowledge. When students learn a sanitized version of history, they develop a distorted framework for understanding current events and evaluating government actions. They may struggle to recognize patterns of oppression or abuse of power because they lack the historical context to identify them.

The False Promise of "National Unity"

Defenders of state-controlled education often argue that a carefully managed historical narrative promotes national unity and social stability. They claim that exposing young people to the full complexity of historical conflicts and injustices might foster division or undermine patriotism. This argument, however, reveals a fundamental misunderstanding of both education and patriotism.

True national unity cannot be built on foundations of historical fiction. When people eventually discover the gaps between official narratives and reality – as they inevitably do in our interconnected world – the result is often a profound crisis of trust. The very social stability that controlled education supposedly protects becomes more fragile, not less. Moreover, this approach fundamentally underestimates young people's capacity to engage with complex and challenging information. Students can handle historical ambiguity and moral complexity. In fact, wrestling with difficult historical truths helps develop critical thinking skills and emotional maturity that are essential for civic participation.

The Cost to Civil Society

When education becomes a tool for ideological control, the damage extends far beyond the classroom. A society whose citizens have been trained to accept official narratives without question becomes vulnerable to manipulation in all spheres of life. The habits of mind that make democratic governance possible – critical thinking, evidence-based reasoning, and moral judgment – are systematically undermined.

This creates a self-reinforcing cycle. Citizens who haven't learned to question authority or evaluate competing claims become less capable of resisting future attempts at manipulation. The space for genuine public discourse shrinks, as fewer people possess the intellectual tools needed to engage in meaningful debate about social and political issues.

The Global Dimension

In our interconnected world, state control of historical narratives has implications that reach across borders. When different countries teach contradictory versions of shared historical events, it becomes harder to build mutual understanding or resolve conflicts. Historical grievances fester because there's no shared foundation of facts upon which to base dialogue.

This dynamic is particularly visible in regions with a history of conflict. When each side teaches its own version of history, emphasizing its own victimhood and minimizing its own transgressions, the result is generations of citizens who find it almost impossible to understand each other's perspectives or work toward reconciliation.

The Role of Technology

The internet era has complicated state efforts to control historical narratives, but it hasn't eliminated them. Instead, many authoritarian regimes have adapted their approaches, combining traditional censorship with sophisticated information control strategies. They flood the internet with their preferred narratives, use social media to discredit alternative viewpoints, and create uncertainty about what information can be trusted. However, technology also offers hope. The availability of alternative sources of historical information makes it harder to maintain complete control over national narratives.

Young people, in particular, often find ways to access banned information and share it with others. This creates opportunities for grassroots resistance to official historical narratives.

Standardization Over Critical Thinking

In modern education systems, the emphasis on standardized testing has often come at the expense of creativity and critical thinking. When students are taught to memorize answers rather than question problems, the result is a generation of individuals who are adept at following instructions but lack the ability to think independently.

The Funding Problem

In many parts of the world, the potential of education to combat ignorance is undermined by chronic underfunding. Public schools, particularly in low-income areas, often lack the resources to provide a quality education. This disparity perpetuates cycles of poverty and ignorance, as students from disadvantaged backgrounds are denied the opportunities afforded to their wealthier peers.

Moreover, underfunded schools struggle to attract and retain qualified teachers. Educators, who should be at the forefront of shaping young minds, are often overworked, underpaid, and undervalued. In such conditions, even the most dedicated teachers can only do so much.

Ideological Battles in the Classroom

In recent years, education has become a battleground for ideological wars. Debates over curriculum content ranging from the teaching of evolution and climate change to discussions of race, gender, and history, reflect broader societal conflicts. For instance, the "critical race theory" controversy in the United States has sparked heated debates over how history and systemic racism should be taught in schools.

On one side are those who argue that an honest reckoning with history is essential for progress; on the other, those who see such discussions as divisive or unpatriotic. These battles illustrate how education is rarely neutral. The content of curricula, the structure of schools, and even the methods of teaching are shaped by cultural, political, and economic forces.

The Power of Lifelong Learning

Finally, education should not end at graduation. Lifelong learning through books, workshops, online courses, and personal exploration, allows individuals to adapt to a rapidly changing world and remain intellectually engaged. Cultivating a culture of lifelong learning can help society resist the pull of ignorance and embrace the joy of discovery. Education is neither inherently good nor inherently bad. It is a tool, and like any tool, its value lies in how it is used. When wielded wisely, it can illuminate the darkest corners of ignorance and guide humanity toward a brighter future. When misused, it can entrench ignorance and perpetuate cycles of oppression. The challenge, then, is to ensure that education serves as a beacon of enlightenment, not a weapon of control.

Chapter 9

The Erosion of Critical Thinking

I know of no time in human history where ignorance was
better than knowledge.
- Neil deGrasse Tyson

In an era defined by unprecedented access to
information and technological advancement, we find
ourselves facing a paradoxical crisis: the erosion of
critical thinking. This decline in our ability to analyze,
evaluate, and form reasoned judgments threatens the
very foundations of our intellectual and social progress.
As artificial intelligence (AI) increasingly permeates our
daily lives, offering quick solutions and easy answers, we
risk becoming intellectually complacent, relying more on
emotional reasoning and pre-packaged responses than on
our own analytical faculties.

The implications of this trend are far-reaching and
profound, touching every aspect of our society from
education and politics to scientific inquiry and personal

decision-making. This erosion of critical thinking skills not only hampers our ability to navigate the complexities of the modern world but also leaves us vulnerable to manipulation and misinformation. As we delve into this issue, we must consider the multifaceted nature of the problem, its root causes, and potential solutions to reinvigorate our collective capacity for reasoned thought.

The State of Critical Thinking Today

Recent studies and observations paint a concerning picture of the state of critical thinking in our society. A study conducted by Dr. Michael Gerlich at the SBS Swiss Business School revealed a strong negative correlation between the use of AI tools and critical thinking skills. This finding suggests that as we increasingly rely on AI for cognitive tasks, our ability to think critically diminishes. The study found that participants who reported higher use of AI scored worse on measures of critical thinking, with a correlation coefficient of -0.68 ($p < 0.001$).

This decline is not limited to academic settings but extends to professional environments as well. In recruitment efforts, employers have noticed a trend where candidates submit AI-generated responses to case studies, lacking the depth and genuine insight that comes from critical analysis. This reliance on AI-generated content signals a shift away from engaging with problems critically to accepting pre-packaged answers, a trend that is alarming for its implications on innovation and problem-solving in the workplace.

Moreover, the erosion of critical thinking is evident in public discourse, where emotional reasoning often trumps logical analysis. The rise of social media and the 24-hour news cycle has created an environment where quick, emotionally charged responses are valued over thoughtful, nuanced analysis. This shift has significant implications for our ability to address complex societal issues and make informed decisions as citizens.

The Role of AI in Cognitive Offloading

The rapid integration of AI into our daily lives has led to a phenomenon known as cognitive offloading, where individuals rely on external tools to reduce mental effort. While this can increase efficiency in certain tasks, it also poses risks to our cognitive abilities, particularly our critical thinking skills.

AI tools, from virtual assistants to complex decision support systems, are designed to make our lives easier by handling cognitive tasks on our behalf. However, this convenience comes at a cost. As we offload more of our thinking to AI, we risk atrophying our own analytical abilities. Dr. Gerlich's research suggests that when AI frees up cognitive resources, users typically don't use this extra mental capacity for problem-solving or creative endeavors. Instead, they often engage in passive consumption, such as watching streaming services or browsing social media – activities that are themselves often curated by AI algorithms.

This cycle of dependence on AI for cognitive tasks and the subsequent use of freed-up mental resources for passive activities creates a feedback loop that can significantly impair our critical thinking abilities over time. The danger lies not in the use of AI itself, but in our growing reliance on it for tasks that once required active engagement of our analytical faculties.

The Rise of Emotional Reasoning

Alongside the decline in critical thinking skills, we've witnessed a rise in emotional reasoning – a cognitive distortion where individuals believe something is true simply because it feels true. This trend is particularly concerning as it often leads to poor decision-making and can be easily exploited for manipulation.

Emotional reasoning can manifest in various ways. For instance, an individual feeling anxious about a work project might assume, without evidence, that their colleagues are disappointed with their progress. This assumption, based solely on emotional state rather than objective reality, can lead to a self-fulfilling prophecy, negatively impacting performance and perpetuating a cycle of negative thoughts.

The prevalence of emotional reasoning in public discourse is equally troubling. In debates on complex issues, we often see arguments based on feelings rather than facts, with individuals dismissing contradictory evidence because it doesn't align with their emotional stance. This approach not only hinders productive dialogue but also makes it difficult to address societal challenges effectively. It's important to note that emotions are not inherently detrimental to critical thinking. In fact, they can play a crucial role in moral reasoning and decision-making.

The problem arises when emotions become the primary or sole basis for judgments, overshadowing logical analysis and evidence-based reasoning.

The Impact of Technology and Social Media

The digital age has transformed how we access and process information, with significant implications for critical thinking. While the internet has democratized access to knowledge, it has also created an environment where misinformation can spread rapidly and where the sheer volume of available information can be overwhelming.

Social media platforms, in particular, have had a profound impact on how we engage with information and form opinions. These platforms often prioritize content that elicits strong emotional responses, as this drives engagement. Consequently, users are frequently exposed to polarizing viewpoints and sensationalized content, which can reinforce biases and hinder objective analysis.

Moreover, the algorithmic curation of content on these platforms can create echo chambers, where individuals are primarily exposed to information that aligns with their existing beliefs. This lack of exposure to diverse perspectives can severely limit one's ability to think critically about complex issues.

The "Google effect," or digital amnesia, is another technological phenomenon impacting our cognitive abilities. As we increasingly rely on search engines to access information, we're less likely to retain that information ourselves. While this frees up cognitive resources, it also means we're less likely to engage deeply with information, potentially hampering our ability to analyze and synthesize ideas critically.

Educational Challenges

The education system plays a crucial role in developing critical thinking skills, yet it faces significant challenges in this area. Traditional educational models often emphasize rote learning and standardized testing over the development of analytical and problem-solving skills. This approach can leave students ill-equipped to navigate the complexities of the modern world.

Furthermore, the integration of technology in education, while offering many benefits, also presents challenges. The ease with which students can access information online can discourage deep engagement with material and independent analysis. There's a risk that students become adept at finding information quickly but struggle to evaluate its credibility or synthesize it into original insights.

The rise of AI tools in education adds another layer of complexity. While these tools can enhance learning in many ways, there's a danger that over-reliance on them could hinder the development of critical thinking skills. Educators face the challenge of teaching students how to use AI tools effectively while still fostering independent analytical abilities.

The Role of Media and Information Literacy

In an age of information overload and widespread misinformation, media and information literacy have become crucial components of critical thinking. The ability to evaluate sources, recognize bias, and distinguish fact from opinion is essential for navigating the modern information landscape.

However, studies suggest that many individuals, particularly younger generations, struggle with these skills. A lack of media literacy can lead to the uncritical acceptance of information from unreliable sources, making individuals vulnerable to manipulation and reinforcing the cycle of emotional reasoning over critical analysis.

Addressing this issue requires a concerted effort to integrate media and information literacy into educational curricula and public awareness campaigns. Teaching individuals how to critically evaluate the information they encounter online and in traditional media is essential for fostering a society capable of reasoned discourse and informed decision-making.

The Implications for Democracy and Civil Discourse

The erosion of critical thinking skills has profound implications for democratic societies. A well-functioning democracy relies on an informed citizenry capable of analyzing complex issues and making reasoned decisions. When critical thinking declines, and emotional reasoning predominates, the quality of public discourse suffers, and the electorate becomes more susceptible to manipulation and demagoguery.

We've seen evidence of this in recent years, with the rise of populist movements and the spread of conspiracy theories. These phenomena often thrive in environments where emotional appeals trump logical analysis, and where complex issues are reduced to simplistic, often false, narratives.

Moreover, the decline in critical thinking skills can exacerbate political polarization. When individuals lack the ability to critically evaluate information and consider diverse perspectives, they're more likely to entrench themselves in ideological echo chambers, further widening societal divides.

The Economic and Professional Impact

The erosion of critical thinking skills also has significant implications for the economy and professional world. In an increasingly complex and rapidly changing global economy, the ability to analyze information, solve problems, and adapt to new situations is crucial for both individual and organizational success.

Employers consistently rank critical thinking among the most desirable skills in job candidates. However, as noted earlier, there's growing concern about the decline of these skills among job applicants. This gap between the skills demanded by the job market and those possessed by the workforce could have serious economic consequences, potentially hampering innovation and productivity.

Furthermore, as AI and automation continue to transform the job market, critical thinking skills become even more valuable. While routine cognitive tasks can be increasingly automated, the ability to think critically, creatively solve problems, and make nuanced judgments remains a uniquely human capability. Cultivating these skills is therefore essential for maintaining employability in the face of technological change.

Potential Solutions and Ways Forward

Addressing the erosion of critical thinking requires a multifaceted approach involving education, technology, and societal change. Here are some potential strategies:

- Educational Reform: Revamping educational curricula to place greater emphasis on critical thinking, problem-solving, and media literacy. This could involve more project-based learning, debates, and exercises that encourage students to analyze information critically.

- Responsible AI Integration: Developing guidelines for the responsible integration of AI tools in education and professional settings. This should focus on using AI to augment human thinking rather than replace it.

- Media Literacy Programs: Implementing widespread media and information literacy programs, both in schools and for the general public, to improve people's ability to critically evaluate information.

- Promoting Diverse Perspectives: Encouraging exposure to diverse viewpoints and fostering environments where respectful disagreement and debate are valued.

- Mindfulness and Emotional Intelligence: Teaching techniques to help individuals recognize and manage their emotions, reducing the impact of emotional reasoning on decision-making.

- Critical Thinking in the Workplace: Encouraging businesses to prioritize critical thinking skills in hiring and professional development programs.

- Public Awareness Campaigns: Launching campaigns to raise awareness about the importance of critical thinking and the dangers of uncritical acceptance of information.

- Research and Development: Investing in research to better understand the impacts of technology on cognition and develop tools that enhance rather than diminish critical thinking abilities.

The Role of Individual Responsibility

While systemic changes are crucial, individual responsibility also plays a vital role in cultivating critical thinking skills. Each person can take steps to enhance their analytical abilities and resist the erosion of critical thinking:

- Practice Active Reading: Engage deeply with texts, questioning assumptions and evaluating arguments.

- Seek Diverse Perspectives: Actively seek out viewpoints that challenge your own beliefs.

- Limit Social Media Consumption: Be mindful of time spent on social media and actively curate a diverse information diet.

- Engage in Reflective Thinking: Regularly set aside time for reflection and analysis of your own thoughts and decisions.

- Learn About Cognitive Biases: Educate yourself about common cognitive biases and how they can influence your thinking.

- Practice Mindfulness: Develop mindfulness techniques to better recognize and manage emotional responses.

- Engage in Constructive Debates: Participate in respectful discussions on complex topics, focusing on understanding rather than winning arguments.

- Continuous Learning: Commit to lifelong learning, constantly challenging yourself to acquire new knowledge and skills.

Rekindling the Flame of Reason

The erosion of critical thinking represents a significant challenge to our society, threatening our ability to navigate the complexities of the modern world and make informed decisions. As we increasingly rely on AI and other technologies to augment our cognitive abilities, we must be vigilant in preserving and cultivating our capacity for independent, analytical thought. The path forward requires a delicate balance.

We must harness the benefits of technological advancement while safeguarding against its potential to diminish our cognitive abilities. This involves not only systemic changes in education and public discourse but also a renewed commitment to critical thinking at the individual level. By recognizing the value of both emotional intelligence and logical reasoning, we can work towards a more balanced approach to decision-making and problem-solving. Critical thinking should not be seen as the cold, detached analysis often portrayed in popular culture, but as a rich, nuanced process that incorporates both reason and empathy.

As we face unprecedented global challenges, from climate change to technological disruption, the ability to think critically has never been more important. It is the cornerstone of innovation, the foundation of democracy, and the key to personal and societal progress.

The erosion of critical thinking is not an inevitable consequence of technological advancement. With conscious effort and strategic interventions, we can reverse this trend and foster a society that values and practices reasoned analysis. By doing so, we not only enhance our individual capabilities but also strengthen our collective ability to address the complex issues of our time.

In the end, the cultivation of critical thinking is not just an academic exercise or a professional skill – it is a fundamental aspect of what it means to be human. It is our ability to question, to analyze, to imagine alternatives, and to make reasoned judgments that sets us apart and drives our progress as a species. As we navigate the challenges of the 21st century, rekindling the flame of reason and nurturing our capacity for critical thought must be a priority for individuals, institutions, and society as a whole.

Chapter 10

Religion & Rejection of Reason

Science makes no claim to infallibility; it leaves that claim to be made by theology. - John Burroughs

Few forces in human history have shaped society as profoundly as religion. It has inspired breathtaking art, fostered communities, and provided solace to billions. Religious faith has inspired some of humanity's greatest artistic and architectural achievements. The soaring spires of Gothic cathedrals, the intricate geometric patterns of Islamic art, and the serene beauty of Buddhist temples all stand as testaments to how spiritual devotion can fuel creative expression. The Sistine Chapel ceiling, Bach's Mass in B Minor, and countless other master-works were born from religious inspiration. At the same time, religion has often stood in opposition to reason, science, and progress. This complex duality has profoundly shaped civilizations, leaving an indelible mark on art, science, philosophy, and social structures.

Beyond aesthetics, religious institutions have historically served as crucial social anchors. Places of worship have functioned as community centers, providing education, charity, and social services. Religious communities have offered support networks, shared values, and a sense of belonging that helps many people navigate life's challenges. During times of hardship, faith has provided hope and resilience to countless individuals.

Faith vs. Reason: A Historical Struggle

The tension between faith and reason is as old as civilization itself. In ancient Greece, philosophers like Socrates, Plato, and Aristotle championed rational inquiry, while mythological explanations dominated popular thought. Early religions often relied on supernatural narratives to explain natural phenomena, providing answers in the absence of scientific understanding.

However, as reason began to challenge religious orthodoxy, conflict arose. One of the most iconic examples is the trial of Galileo Galilei in 1633. Galileo's support for the heliocentric model of the solar system—a theory based on observation and evidence—was deemed heretical by the Catholic Church. His forced recantation and house arrest became a symbol of religion's resistance to scientific progress.

While not all religions opposed intellectual advancement, many sought to control knowledge to maintain authority. This historical pattern demonstrates how religion, when wielded as a tool of power, can suppress inquiry and critical thought.

Modern-Day Rejections of Reason

In an era defined by unprecedented scientific and technological advancement, it is both perplexing and alarming to witness the persistent rejection of reason by certain religious movements. This 21st-century manifestation of the age-old conflict between faith and science poses significant challenges to our society's progress and well-being. The rejection of scientific consensus by some religious groups is not merely a matter of personal belief; it has far-reaching consequences that affect us all. From climate change denial to the anti-vaccination movement, these ideological stances threaten public health, environmental sustainability, and our collective future.

Take, for example, the ongoing debate surrounding evolution. Despite overwhelming scientific evidence supporting the theory of evolution, some religious groups continue to push for the teaching of creationism or "intelligent design" in science classrooms. This not only undermines the quality of science education but also blurs the line between religious belief and empirical fact.

Similarly, the rejection of climate science by certain religious conservatives has hindered crucial efforts to address global warming. By framing environmental concerns as contrary to religious values or divine will, these groups have contributed to political gridlock on climate action, potentially jeopardizing the future of our planet.

The anti-vaccination movement, often fueled by a mix of religious objections and pseudo-scientific claims, presents another clear danger. The resurgence of preventable diseases due to declining vaccination rates is a stark reminder of the real-world consequences when faith-based rejection of science goes mainstream.

It's important to note that this is not an indictment of all religious belief. Many religious individuals and organizations embrace scientific understanding, seeing no conflict between their faith and reason. The problem arises when religious dogma is used to dismiss empirical evidence and expert consensus. The solution to this challenge lies not in attacking religion itself, but in promoting scientific literacy and critical thinking skills. We must foster an environment where faith and reason can coexist, where religious beliefs are respected but not allowed to override scientific fact in matters of public policy and education.

Educational institutions have a crucial role to play in this effort. By emphasizing the scientific method, evidence-based reasoning, and the ability to distinguish between fact and opinion, we can equip future generations with the tools to navigate an increasingly complex world. Moreover, religious leaders who embrace science should be amplified and supported. These voices can serve as powerful mediators, demonstrating that faith and reason need not be at odds. As we face global challenges that require collective action based on scientific understanding – from pandemics to climate change – we cannot afford to let the rejection of reason gain further ground.

The stakes are simply too high. While respecting freedom of belief, we must stand firm in defending the role of science and reason in shaping our shared reality. The future of our society depends on our ability to bridge the divide between faith and fact, fostering a culture where both spiritual beliefs and scientific truths can inform our understanding of the world.

The Role of Dogma

At the heart of religion's rejection of reason lies dogma: a set of principles accepted as unquestionably true. Dogma discourages questioning and critical examination, demanding adherence even when evidence suggests otherwise. One striking example is the resistance to LGBTQ+ rights by certain religious institutions. Despite growing societal acceptance and scientific understanding of sexuality and gender, many religious groups cling to doctrines that marginalize LGBTQ+ individuals. The harm caused by this dogmatic stance—ranging from mental health struggles to social exclusion—is a stark reminder of how rigid beliefs can perpetuate ignorance and suffering.

Dogma's power lies in its ability to create certainty. In a world filled with uncertainty, this can be comforting. But certainty without evidence is a fragile foundation, easily manipulated by those seeking to control others.

The Other Side of Faith

Not all religion opposes reason. Many religious traditions encourage intellectual inquiry, ethical reflection, and a deeper understanding of the human condition. For instance, Islamic scholars during the Golden Age of Islam made significant contributions to science, medicine, and mathematics. Likewise, figures like Martin Luther King Jr. used religious principles to advocate for social justice and equality. Similarly, many prominent religious leaders in South Africa were at the forefront of the fight against Apartheid. Figures like Desmond Tutu, Dr Allen Boesak, Frank Chikane, and Beyers Naudé used their moral authority to condemn apartheid as a crime against humanity and helped mobilize support for the anti-apartheid movement.

They played crucial roles in opposing the system

through peaceful means, often at great personal risk. Faith and reason are not inherently incompatible. They can coexist, provided that faith remains a personal journey rather than a societal mandate. Problems arise when religious beliefs are imposed on others, particularly when they conflict with evidence-based knowledge.

Religious Manipulation of Ignorance

Religion, like education, can be wielded as a tool for control. Throughout history, religious leaders have exploited ignorance to maintain power, often discouraging literacy and independent thought among followers. Consider the Middle Ages, when the Catholic Church restricted access to the Bible by keeping it in Latin, a language most people could not read. This ensured that religious interpretation remained the exclusive domain of the clergy, reinforcing their authority.

Today, similar tactics can be seen in some religious sects that discourage questioning, isolate members from external influences, and punish dissent. These practices create echo chambers, where ignorance is not only tolerated but enforced.

While acknowledging these historical abuses, we must also recognize the many instances where religion has been a force for education, enlightenment, and social progress. Many religious institutions have been at the forefront of establishing schools, universities, and hospitals, contributing significantly to the advancement of knowledge and human welfare.

Balancing Faith and Critical Thinking

In our increasingly polarized world, the tension between

faith and reason continues to be a source of conflict, misunderstanding, and division. The challenge before us is not to eradicate faith or to dismiss reason, but to foster a society where these two fundamental aspects of human experience can coexist harmoniously. This requires a delicate balance, one that respects the deeply personal nature of faith while upholding the importance of evidence-based reasoning in our shared public life.

At the heart of this challenge lies the concept of intellectual humility. This virtue, often overlooked in our culture of certainty and polarization, is crucial for bridging the gap between faith and reason. Intellectual humility involves recognizing the limitations of our own knowledge and being open to the possibility that we might be wrong. It's about approaching our beliefs – whether religious or secular – with a sense of tentativeness and a willingness to revise them in light of new evidence or perspectives.

For those with strong religious convictions, intellectual humility means acknowledging that faith is, by definition, a belief in something that cannot be proven empirically. It means recognizing that while one's faith may provide profound personal meaning and guidance, it should not be used as a substitute for evidence-based reasoning in matters that affect the broader society. This doesn't diminish the value or importance of faith; rather, it places it in its proper context as a personal, spiritual matter.

For those who prioritize reason and scientific evidence, intellectual humility involves acknowledging the limitations of human knowledge and the ever-evolving nature of scientific understanding. It means recognizing that while the scientific method is our best tool for understanding the physical world, it may not provide answers to all of life's questions, particularly those related to meaning, purpose, and morality.

The Personal Nature of Faith

One of the key principles in fostering coexistence between faith and reason is recognizing that faith is inherently personal. Religious beliefs are deeply rooted in individual experiences, cultural backgrounds, and personal interpretations of spiritual truths. As such, they should be respected as a matter of personal choice and freedom of conscience.

However, this personal nature of faith also means that it should not be imposed on others or used as a basis for public policy that affects all members of society, regardless of their beliefs. When faith-based views are presented in the public sphere, they should be subject to the same scrutiny and debate as any other ideas, and should be supported by reasoning and evidence that can be understood and evaluated by all, regardless of their religious background.

The Role of Evidence-Based Reasoning

While respecting the personal nature of faith, we must also uphold the importance of evidence-based reasoning, particularly in matters of public policy, education, and scientific inquiry. Evidence-based reasoning provides a common ground for people of different beliefs to come together and make decisions based on shared, verifiable information.

This approach is crucial in addressing the complex challenges of our time, from climate change to public health crises. When making decisions that affect the entire society, we need to rely on methods that can be tested, verified, and replicated, rather than on personal beliefs that cannot be empirically proven.

Separating Church and State:

The separation of church and state stands as a cornerstone of modern democratic societies, ensuring religious freedom while safeguarding rational governance. This principle, far from being an attack on faith, serves to protect both the integrity of religious institutions and the efficacy of public policy. As we navigate the complex landscape of the 21st century, the importance of maintaining this separation has never been more apparent.

At its core, the separation of church and state is about creating a neutral public sphere where all citizens, regardless of their religious beliefs or lack thereof, can participate equally. Paradoxically, the separation of church and state is one of the strongest protections for religious freedom. When the government remains neutral on matters of faith, it creates a space where all religions can flourish without fear of persecution or discrimination.

This principle protects minority religions from the tyranny of the majority. In a diverse society, allowing any one religion to dominate public policy would inevitably lead to the marginalization of other faiths.

Moreover, keeping religion separate from government protects faith itself from corruption by political power. When religious institutions become too closely aligned with the state, they risk losing their spiritual focus and becoming mere tools of political influence. Religion's power lies in its ability to inspire hope, provide meaning, and foster community. Reason's power lies in its ability to uncover truths, solve problems, and improve lives. Together, they have the potential to enrich humanity in ways that neither can achieve alone. However, this requires an acknowledgement of their respective roles. When religion oversteps into the domain of reason, conflict arises.

Chapter 11

Technology: Enlightenment or Enabler?

It has become appallingly obvious that our technology has exceeded our humanity. - Albert Einstein

Technology is a double-edged sword. It has transformed human civilization, empowering individuals with knowledge, enhancing communication, and solving complex problems. At the same time, it has given rise to unprecedented levels of misinformation, manipulation, and intellectual laziness. Technology has become both an unparalleled enabler of enlightenment and a dangerous amplifier of ignorance. By examining the role of social media, algorithms, artificial intelligence, and digital addiction, we can understand why technology's promise of knowledge remains so elusive. At its best, technology represents the fulfillment of humanity's quest for knowledge. The invention of the printing press democratized information, breaking the stranglehold of elites who controlled access to knowledge. Centuries later, the internet has revolutionized how we acquire and share information.

Never before has so much knowledge been so readily accessible. In seconds, anyone with an internet connection can research scientific breakthroughs, enrol in online courses, or access libraries of human achievement. The digital age has the potential to fulfil the Enlightenment ideals of reason and progress. And yet, we find ourselves drowning in a sea of misinformation, conspiracy theories, and digital distractions.

The same tools that empower us can also mislead, overwhelm, and manipulate. In the grand tapestry of human progress, technology stands as both our greatest achievement and our most perplexing paradox. While we celebrate its capacity to democratize knowledge and connect minds across continents, we must confront an uncomfortable truth: the same tools that promised to usher in an age of enlightenment have become powerful enablers of willful ignorance and ideological entrenchment.

Consider the smartphone in your pocket – a device with more computing power than what guided humans to the moon. It offers instant access to humanity's collective knowledge, from ancient philosophies to cutting-edge scientific discoveries. Yet, increasingly, these pocket-sized oracles serve not as gateways to enlightenment but as mirrors, reflecting back our preexisting beliefs and biases with algorithmic precision. The promise of the information age was that knowledge would flow freely, washing away the shores of ignorance like a digital tide. Instead, we've witnessed the rise of what I call "curated ignorance" – a phenomenon where individuals actively use technology to construct elaborate frameworks that justify and reinforce their existing worldviews.

Social media algorithms, designed to maximize engagement, have become sophisticated enablers of this process, creating echo chambers where dissenting voices are systematically filtered out, and confirmation bias reigns supreme. But the relationship between technology and ignorance runs deeper than mere algorithmic amplification. Technology has fundamentally altered how we process and validate information. In an era where deep fakes are increasingly sophisticated and misinformation spreads at the speed of a click, the very notion of truth has become malleable. We find ourselves in the peculiar position of having access to more facts than ever before, while simultaneously losing our collective ability to agree on what constitutes a fact.

The fault, however, lies not in our technologies but in how we've chosen to wield them. The same platforms that can spread conspiracy theories can also host vibrant intellectual discussions. The same search engines that can lead users down rabbit holes of extremism can also guide them to peer-reviewed research and thoughtful analysis.

The critical difference lies not in the tools themselves but in the mental frameworks we bring to their use. This brings us to a crucial question: How do we transform technology from an enabler of ignorance back into an instrument of enlightenment? The answer, I believe, lies in re-imagining our relationship with these tools. We must shift from passive consumption to active engagement, from seeking confirmation to embracing challenge, from digital tribalism to intellectual curiosity.

Consider the contrast between two approaches to using technology for learning. The first user, encountering an idea that challenges their beliefs, immediately seeks out information that confirms their existing viewpoint. They share content without verification, block dissenting voices, and gradually construct an impenetrable bubble of self-reinforcing beliefs. The second user, facing the same challenging idea, uses technology to explore multiple perspectives, seeks out primary sources, engages with contrary viewpoints, and approaches information with healthy skepticism.

The difference between these approaches illustrates a fundamental truth: technology amplifies our intellectual tendencies. For the curious, it becomes a tool of enlightenment; for the dogmatic, it becomes a weapon of ignorance. The technology itself is neutral – it's our approach to its use that determines its impact on our understanding of the world.

The Attention Economy and the Cult of Ignorance

Perhaps the most insidious effect of modern technology is its role in creating what some scholars call the "attention economy." In this paradigm, our attention becomes a commodity to be captured and monetized by tech companies and content creators.

This has led to the proliferation of clickbait headlines, addictive app designs, and content optimized for quick consumption rather than deep understanding. The result is a culture that often prioritizes entertainment and instant gratification over intellectual growth and critical analysis. In this environment, ignorance can thrive. It's easier to share a meme or retweet a provocative statement than to read a long-form article or engage in substantive debate. The cult of ignorance finds fertile ground in this landscape, where complex issues are reduced to simplistic slogans and tribal affiliations often trump factual accuracy.

The Role of Big Tech

The tech giants that dominate our digital landscape bear significant responsibility for these trends. Their business models, often reliant on advertising revenue, incentivise engagement over enlightenment. While companies like Facebook, Google, and X (Twitter) have made efforts to combat misinformation and promote authoritative sources, critics argue that these measures are often too little, too late. The immense power wielded by these companies raises important questions about the privatization of the public sphere. As more of our discourse moves online, we must grapple with the implications of having a handful of corporations effectively controlling the platforms for global communication and information dissemination.

Reclaiming Technology for Enlightenment

Despite these challenges, it would be a mistake to view technology as inherently detrimental to critical thinking and enlightenment. The key lies in how we choose to use and shape these tools. Education systems must evolve to emphasize digital literacy and critical thinking skills. Students should be taught not just how to use technology, but how to evaluate information sources, recognize bias, and engage in constructive online discourse.

Individuals can take steps to curate their digital environments more consciously, seeking out diverse perspectives and prioritizing quality information sources over sensationalism. Practicing "digital mindfulness" – being intentional about our technology use and taking regular breaks from screens – can help combat information overload and preserve our capacity for deep thinking.

Policymakers and tech companies must work together to create a digital ecosystem that promotes enlightenment over ignorance. This could involve rethinking algorithmic design to prioritize diverse viewpoints, implementing stronger measures against misinformation, and exploring new business models that don't rely on capturing and monetizing user attention.

Technology, like any tool, is neutral; its impact depends on how we choose to use it. While it has the potential to usher in a new age of enlightenment, it can also enable the spread of ignorance and fanaticism. The challenge before us is to harness the power of technology to foster critical thinking, promote diverse perspectives, and combat the cult of ignorance. As we navigate this digital age, we must remain vigilant, continuously questioning not just the information we consume, but also the systems and platforms through which we access it.

By doing so, we can work towards a future where technology serves as a true enabler of enlightenment, empowering us to think more critically, engage more deeply, and ultimately build a more informed and thoughtful society.

It requires a collective effort – from tech companies, policymakers, educators, and individual users – to reshape our digital landscape. Only then can we ensure that technology fulfills its promise as a force for enlightenment rather than an enabler of ignorance.

As we navigate this digital age, we must recognize that technology's role in either enlightening or enabling ignorance ultimately depends on our chosen relationship with it. Will we use these powerful tools to challenge our assumptions and expand our understanding? Or will we allow them to calcify our biases and deepen our divisions? The answer to this question will determine not just our individual relationship with knowledge but the very fabric of our shared reality.

In an era where technology mediates so much of our understanding of the world, learning to use these tools wisely isn't just an intellectual exercise – it's a civic responsibility.

Chapter 12

Political Exploitation of Ignorance

The ignorance of one voter in a democracy
impairs the security of all. - John F. Kennedy

Politics, like technology, wields immense power to shape society. While democratic systems are built on the ideal of an informed electorate, history has repeatedly shown how ignorance is exploited to manipulate the masses, consolidate power, and perpetuate inequality.

The parallels between politics and technology in their capacity to influence and transform society are striking. Both have the potential to empower individuals and communities, fostering progress and innovation. Yet, both can also be wielded as tools of control and oppression when placed in the wrong hands or used without proper safeguards.

Democratic systems, in their purest form, are designed to give voice to the people, allowing them to participate in the decision-making processes that govern their lives. The foundation of this system rests on the assumption of an informed citizenry, capable of making rational choices based on a clear understanding of the issues at hand. As Thomas Jefferson famously stated, "An educated citizenry is a vital requisite for our survival as a free people."

However, the reality often falls short of this ideal. Throughout history, we have witnessed how political actors have exploited ignorance and misinformation to further their own agendas. This manipulation takes many forms, from the spread of propaganda and false narratives to the deliberate suppression of information that might challenge existing power structures.

The exploitation of ignorance in politics is not a new phenomenon. Ancient rulers and modern dictators alike have recognized that a populace kept in the dark is easier to control. In the words of Noam Chomsky, "The general population doesn't know what's happening, and it doesn't even know that it doesn't know." This state of affairs allows those in power to shape public opinion and behaviour to their advantage.

One of the most insidious aspects of this exploitation is its self-perpetuating nature. By keeping citizens uninformed or misinformed, those in power can maintain their grip on authority, which in turn allows them to further control the flow of information. This vicious cycle can lead to the erosion of democratic principles and the consolidation of power in the hands of a few.

Moreover, the exploitation of ignorance often serves to perpetuate existing inequalities within society. By manipulating public opinion, those in power can maintain systems that benefit certain groups at the expense of others. This can manifest in various ways, from economic policies that favour the wealthy to social structures that reinforce racial or gender disparities.

In the modern era, the challenges posed by the exploitation of ignorance in politics have been amplified by technological advancements. The rise of social media and the 24-hour news cycle has created an information landscape that is both vast and fragmented. While this has the potential to democratize information, it has also made it easier for misinformation to spread rapidly and for echo chambers to form, reinforcing existing biases and beliefs.

The consequences of this exploitation are far-reaching and profound. When citizens are unable to make informed decisions, the very foundations of democracy are undermined. Policies may be enacted that go against the best interests of the majority, and leaders may be elected based on false promises or manufactured fears rather than their ability to govern effectively.

Furthermore, the exploitation of ignorance can lead to a breakdown in social cohesion. When different segments of society operate on entirely different sets of "facts," finding common ground becomes increasingly difficult. This polarization can make it challenging to address pressing societal issues and can even lead to social unrest or violence.

It is crucial to remember that knowledge is power. In the face of those who would exploit ignorance for their own gain, our greatest weapon is an informed and engaged populace.

Ignorance as a Tool of Power

Throughout history, political leaders have understood the value of ignorance as a tool for control. A misinformed populace is easier to manipulate, less likely to resist, and more willing to accept authoritarian rule. The less people know, the more dependent they become on simplified narratives, charismatic leaders, and tribal loyalties.

Historical Precedents:

Bread and Circuses:

The concept of "Bread and Circuses" in ancient Rome, known in Latin as "panem et circenses," was a powerful political strategy employed by Roman emperors to maintain social order and public approval. This phrase, coined by the Roman poet Juvenal in the late 1st or early 2nd century AD, encapsulates a sophisticated system of public welfare and entertainment designed to placate the masses and divert attention from political issues.

The "bread" component of this strategy primarily refers to the grain dole, a system of free or subsidized grain distribution to Roman citizens. This practice evolved over time, becoming increasingly institutionalized under various leaders. Julius Caesar reformed the system in 58 BCE, reducing the number of beneficiaries to make it more efficient and sustainable. Augustus further structured the grain dole in the late 1st century BCE, establishing a more permanent form of state welfare.

The grain was sourced from fertile provinces like Sicily, Egypt, and North Africa, highlighting the strategic importance of these regions to Rome's food security. The grain dole was not merely an act of charity but a calculated political tool. As Suetonius records, Augustus maintained the system despite personal reservations, recognizing its importance in preventing demagogues from using the promise of free grain to gain popular support.

The "circuses" aspect of the phrase referred to various forms of public entertainment, including:

- Gladiatorial contests in the Colosseum, where slaves, criminals, or prisoners of war fought to the death for public amusement.

- Chariot races at the Circus Maximus, which could draw crowds of up to 250,000 spectators.

- Exotic animal fights, theatre performances, and other spectacles.

These entertainments served multiple purposes. They provided an outlet for the public's energy and emotions. They created a sense of shared Roman identity and culture. In addition, they offered a platform for the public to voice opinions, albeit in a controlled environment.

The effectiveness of the "Bread and Circuses" strategy was rooted in its ability to address immediate needs while fostering political complacency.

By providing food and entertainment, emperors could:

- Prevent civil unrest due to hunger or boredom.

- Create a façade of prosperity and generosity.

- Distract the populace from larger issues of corruption, inequality, and loss of political liberty.

Juvenal's critique of this system was prescient, as he saw it as emblematic of the erosion of civic duty and republican values. He lamented that the Roman people, who once actively participated in political and military affairs, had abdicated their responsibilities in exchange for basic sustenance and entertainment.

The long-term consequences of this strategy were significant. It created a dependent population, less likely to challenge authority. It contributed to the financial strain on the empire, as maintaining the grain dole and elaborate spectacles was costly. It may have contributed to the decline of agriculture in Italy, as Augustus himself feared.

The "Bread and Circuses" phenomenon in ancient Rome was a complex and multifaceted strategy that went beyond mere distraction. It was a sophisticated system of social control that addressed real needs while simultaneously undermining civic engagement and republican values. Its legacy serves as a cautionary tale about the potential for governments to use public welfare and entertainment as tools for political manipulation

Nazi Germany:

Joseph Goebbels, as Reich Minister of Propaganda in Nazi Germany, orchestrated one of the most extensive and insidious propaganda campaigns in history. His methods relied heavily on misinformation, fear-mongering, and the exploitation of existing prejudices to manipulate public opinion and justify the Nazi regime's horrific policies.

Goebbels' propaganda machine was multifaceted and pervasive, utilizing various media to spread the Nazi message:

- Control of mass media: Goebbels censored all opposition in the press, radio, and film industries. He ensured that only pro-Nazi content was disseminated, creating an echo chamber of Nazi ideology.

- Exploitation of new technologies: Goebbels pioneered the use of radio and film for propaganda purposes. Cheap "People's Receivers" were distributed widely, and loudspeakers were placed in public spaces to ensure the Nazi message reached every corner of society.

- Visual propaganda: The Nazi swastika and images of Hitler were omnipresent, reinforcing the cult of personality around the Führer.

- Public spectacles: Goebbels organized massive rallies and events, such as book burnings, to create a sense of unity and fervor among the German people.

Central to Goebbels' strategy was the use of scapegoating, particularly targeting Jews and other minorities. This tactic served several purposes:

- Deflecting blame: By framing Jews as responsible for Germany's economic and social problems, the Nazis diverted attention from their own policies and the real causes of these issues.

- Creating a common enemy: The portrayal of Jews as a threat to German society fostered a sense of unity among "true" Germans and justified discriminatory policies.

- Dehumanization: Consistent negative propaganda against Jews and other minorities made it easier for the German public to accept and even participate in their persecution.

Goebbels' approach to propaganda was based on several key principles:

- Simplification and repetition: Complex ideas were reduced to simple, memorable slogans that were repeated ad nauseam.

- Emotional appeal: Propaganda targeted people's emotions, particularly fear and anger, rather than their rational faculties.

- The "big lie" technique: Goebbels believed in the power of audacious falsehoods, asserting that people were more likely to believe a big lie than a small one.

The effectiveness of this propaganda campaign was tragically demonstrated in the German public's acquiescence to, and in some cases active participation in, the escalating persecution of Jews and other minorities. This culminated in the Holocaust, the systematic murder of millions of people.

The legacy of Goebbels' propaganda machine serves as a stark warning about the power of mass media manipulation and the dangers of unchecked government control over information. It underscores the importance of media literacy, critical thinking, and vigilance against scapegoating and hate speech in maintaining a free and just society

McCarthyism:

McCarthyism, named after Senator Joseph McCarthy, was a dark period in American history during the early 1950s that exploited fear of communism to spread paranoia and suppress dissent. This phenomenon had far-reaching consequences that extended beyond McCarthy himself.

Senator McCarthy rose to prominence in 1950 with a speech in Wheeling, West Virginia, where he claimed to have a list of 57 known communists working in the State Department1. Despite never producing credible evidence, McCarthy's accusations gained traction in a climate of Cold War anxiety.

The impact of McCarthyism was severe and wide-ranging:

- Widespread persecution: Thousands of Americans were accused of being communists or sympathizers, often on flimsy or non-existent evidence. Many lost their jobs, were imprisoned, or faced public shame.

- Chilling effect on free speech: McCarthy's tactics created a climate of fear that discouraged open discussion of political ideas. Even mere discussion of communism was seen as dangerous and un-American.

- Hollywood blacklist: Over 300 actors, writers, and directors were denied work in the film industry due to suspected communist sympathies.

- Academic suppression: Universities adapted curricula and professors modified syllabi to avoid controversial topics.

- Government loyalty programs: McCarthy's influence led to the implementation of loyalty tests for government employees.

McCarthy's power began to wane in 1954 during the Army-McCarthy hearings, which were televised nationally. His aggressive tactics were exposed to the public, culminating in Joseph Welch's famous rebuke: "Have you no sense of decency, sir, at long last? Have you left no sense of decency?"

The legacy of McCarthyism serves as a stark reminder of how leaders can exploit ignorance and fear to consolidate power and suppress dissent. By creating a climate of paranoia, McCarthy was able to silence critics and advance his own agenda under the guise of patriotism.

This strategy of exploiting ignorance to obscure true motives and suppress opposition is not unique to McCarthyism. It has been employed by various leaders throughout history to maintain control and deflect scrutiny from their own actions. By fostering an atmosphere of fear and suspicion, such leaders can effectively stifle critical thinking and open debate, allowing them to pursue their agendas with less resistance.

The lessons of McCarthyism underscore the importance of critical thinking, media literacy, and robust protections for civil liberties in maintaining a healthy democracy.

They remind us to be vigilant against those who

would use fear and misinformation to divide and control society.

The Propaganda Playbook

Propaganda is the lifeblood of political exploitation, and modern systems have refined it into an art form. The mechanisms of propaganda work because they appeal not to reason but to emotion, which includes, fear, anger, pride, and belonging.

Simplistic Narratives:

Complex problems like climate change, economic inequality, and public health crises are reduced to oversimplified "us vs. them" narratives. Political leaders frame themselves as saviours and opponents as villains, avoiding nuanced discussions that could expose flaws in their policies.

Fear-Mongering:

Fear is a powerful motivator. Politicians often exploit fear of immigrants, minorities, or foreign adversaries to rally support. For example, during Brexit, false claims about an impending wave of immigration from Turkey were used to stoke fears and sway voters.

Disinformation Campaigns:

In the digital age, misinformation spreads faster than ever. Governments and political actors employ fake news, doctored images, and manipulated statistics to shape public opinion. Political entities frequently use disinformation to discredit opponents, sway elections, and maintain power. Fabricated stories and misleading narratives can inflame social divisions, making it difficult for the public to discern truth from propaganda.

The Basic Education Laws Amendment (BELA) Bill in South Africa

The Basic Education Laws Amendment (BELA) Bill, introduced in South Africa in 2021, and signed into law on the 13th of September 2024, has been one of the most contentious pieces of legislation in recent years. Designed to address critical issues in the country's education system, the Bill has sparked widespread debate, particularly around two key areas: the Afrikaans language policy in schools and the rights of transgender learners regarding bathroom access. However, much of the public discourse surrounding the BELA Bill has been marked by misinterpretation, misinformation, and political opportunism. Opposition parties and interest groups have capitalized on these misunderstandings, organizing protests and framing the Bill as an attack on Afrikaans-speaking communities and traditional values. This article explores how the South African public misinterpreted the BELA Bill, the role of opposition parties in fueling these misconceptions, and the broader implications for education policy in the country.

The BELA Bill: Intent and Key Provisions

The BELA Bill was introduced by the Department of Basic Education to amend existing legislation, including the South African Schools Act (SASA) of 1996 and the Employment of Educators Act of 1998. Its primary objectives were to improve the quality of education, address systemic inequalities, and ensure that schools are more inclusive and responsive to the needs of all learners. Among its many provisions, the Bill sought to:

- Strengthen the role of school governing bodies (SGBs) in determining language policies, while ensuring that these policies align with the constitutional right to basic education.

- Promote inclusivity by addressing the rights of transgender learners, including access to bathrooms that align with their gender identity.

- Enhance accountability by giving the Department of Basic Education greater oversight over school admissions and language policies.

While these provisions were intended to create a more equitable and inclusive education system, they were met with significant resistance, particularly from Afrikaans-speaking communities and conservative groups.

Misinterpretation of the Afrikaans Language Policy

One of the most contentious aspects of the BELA Bill was its perceived threat to Afrikaans-medium education. South Africa has 11 official languages, and the Constitution guarantees the right to receive education in one's language of choice where practicable. Afrikaans-medium schools have long been a cornerstone of the Afrikaans-speaking community, seen as a way to preserve the language and culture in a predominantly English-speaking society.

However, critics of the BELA Bill argued that it

would undermine Afrikaans-medium education by giving the Department of Basic Education the power to override SGB decisions on language policies. They claimed that the Bill would force Afrikaans schools to adopt English as the primary medium of instruction, effectively eroding the rights of Afrikaans-speaking learners.

This interpretation was largely based on a misreading of the Bill's provisions. The BELA Bill did not seek to abolish Afrikaans-medium schools or impose English as the default language. Instead, it aimed to ensure that language policies do not exclude learners from accessing education. For example, if an Afrikaans-medium school had the capacity to accommodate English-speaking learners, it would be required to do so, provided that this did not compromise the quality of education for Afrikaans-speaking learners.

The Department of Basic Education repeatedly clarified that the Bill was not an attack on Afrikaans but rather an attempt to balance the rights of all learners. However, these clarifications were often drowned out by sensationalist media coverage and political rhetoric.

Opposition Parties and the Afrikaans Language Debate

Opposition parties, particularly the Democratic Alliance (DA) and the Freedom Front Plus (FF+), seized on the language policy issue to rally support among Afrikaans-speaking voters. Both parties have historically positioned themselves as defenders of minority rights, and the BELA Bill provided an opportunity to reinforce this narrative.

The FF+, a party with strong ties to the Afrikaans community, framed the Bill as an existential threat to

Afrikaans culture and identity. Party leaders accused the ruling African National Congress (ANC) of pursuing a "cultural genocide" and called on Afrikaans-speaking South Africans to resist the Bill. The DA, while more moderate in its rhetoric, also criticized the Bill, arguing that it undermined the autonomy of SGBs and threatened the diversity of the education system.

These parties organized a series of protests, including a high-profile march to the Union Buildings in Pretoria, the seat of the South African government. The march, which drew thousands of participants, was framed as a defense of Afrikaans-medium education and a rejection of what protesters called "government overreach." While the protest was peaceful, it highlighted the deep-seated anxieties of many Afrikaans-speaking South Africans about the future of their language and culture.

The Clause on Transgender Learners and Bathroom Access

Another highly controversial aspect of the BELA Bill was its provision addressing the rights of transgender learners. The Bill sought to ensure that schools provide safe and inclusive environments for all learners, including those who identify as transgender. Specifically, it required schools to allow transgender learners to use bathrooms that align with their gender identity.

This provision was met with fierce opposition from conservative groups and religious organizations, who argued that it would violate the rights of cisgender learners and undermine traditional values. Critics claimed that the Bill would force schools to allow "biological males" to use girls' bathrooms, posing a threat to the safety and privacy of female learners.

Once again, these criticisms were based on a misinterpretation of the Bill's intent. The provision was not about forcing schools to adopt a one-size-fits-all approach but rather about ensuring that transgender learners are not discriminated against or excluded from essential facilities. The Bill emphasized the importance of consulting with all stakeholders, including parents, learners, and school staff, to develop policies that balance the rights and needs of all learners.

Despite these clarifications, the clause on transgender learners became a lightning rod for controversy, with opponents framing it as evidence of the government's alleged "radical agenda." Social media campaigns and sensationalist headlines further fueled public outrage, leading to widespread misconceptions about the Bill's provisions.

Political Opportunism and the Protest March

The misinterpretation of the BELA Bill was not merely a result of public confusion; it was also a product of deliberate political maneuvering. Opposition parties and interest groups recognized the Bill's potential to galvanize support among specific constituencies and used it to their advantage.

The protest march organized by the Democratic Alliance (DA) and The Freedom Front Plus (FF+) was a case in point. While the march was ostensibly about defending Afrikaans-medium education and protecting the rights of cisgender learners, it also served as a platform for opposition parties to criticize the ANC-led government more broadly. Speakers at the rally accused the government of failing to address pressing issues such as crime, corruption, and unemployment, using the BELA Bill as a symbol of its alleged incompetence and disregard for minority rights.

The march received extensive media coverage, further amplifying the narrative that the BELA Bill was a threat to Afrikaans culture and traditional values. This coverage often failed to provide a balanced perspective, instead focusing on the most sensationalist aspects of the debate.

At the heart of the BELA Bill controversy was a fundamental disconnect between the Bill's actual provisions and the public's perception of them. The Bill sought to address two key issues: the language policy in schools, particularly Afrikaans-medium education, and the rights of transgender learners. Both issues are complex and require nuanced discussion, but instead, they were reduced to soundbites and slogans that played on people's fears and prejudices.

Opposition parties, such as the Democratic Alliance (DA) and the Freedom Front Plus (FF+), were quick to capitalize on this. They framed the Bill as an attack on Afrikaans culture and traditional values, using emotive language to stir up outrage. Religious leaders joined the fray, warning that the Bill would undermine the moral fabric of society. Social media amplified these messages, creating an echo chamber of misinformation and half-truths.

The result was a perfect storm of mass hysteria. Thousands of people took to the streets to protest a Bill they had never read, chanting slogans and waving placards that bore little resemblance to the legislation's actual content. This was not a grassroots movement driven by informed citizens; it was a manufactured outrage, fueled by ignorance and exploited by those with a vested interest in maintaining the status quo.

The Role of Ignorance

Ignorance played a central role in this debacle. Many of the people who protested against the BELA Bill had no idea what it actually said. They relied on second-hand information, often from biased or unreliable sources, and never bothered to read the Bill for themselves. This lack of engagement with the facts allowed misinformation to spread unchecked, creating a distorted narrative that bore little resemblance to reality.

The Danger of Political Opportunism

Opposition parties and religious leaders bear a significant share of the blame for this state of affairs. Instead of fostering a constructive debate, they chose to exploit people's fears and prejudices for political gain. By framing the BELA Bill as a threat to Afrikaans culture and traditional values, they tapped into deep-seated anxieties about identity and belonging, turning a policy discussion into a culture war.

This kind of political opportunism is not new, but it is particularly damaging in a country like South Africa, where the wounds of apartheid are still fresh. By stoking division and mistrust, these actors undermined the possibility of a meaningful dialogue about the future of education in the country. They also reinforced the perception that politics is a zero-sum game, where the goal is not to solve problems but to score points against your opponents.

The Exploitation of Ignorance: A Threat to Democracy

In today's polarized political landscape, the exploitation of ignorance has become a powerful tool for those seeking to manipulate and control the masses. The age-old strategy of "divide and conquer" remains a cornerstone of political manipulation, with leaders exploiting tribalism to pit groups against one another. Whether it's rural versus urban, educated versus working class, or racial divides, keeping the electorate fragmented makes it easier to control.

The rise of "post-truth" politics has only exacerbated this problem. In 2016, Oxford Dictionaries declared "post-truth" their word of the year, signifying a political climate where emotional appeals and personal beliefs overshadow objective facts. This shift has profound implications for the political exploitation of ignorance.

In this post-truth world, facts have become malleable. Politicians make contradictory statements, lie outright, or dismiss inconvenient truths as "fake news" without consequence. The erosion of trust in experts and institutions has left citizens vulnerable to misinformation and manipulation.

The media, unfortunately, often plays a complicit role in this exploitation. Partisan echo chambers, clickbait journalism, and corporate influence shape narratives that align with specific political agendas rather than presenting unbiased information. This polarization ensures viewers receive only one side of the story, further deepening societal divides.

One of the most insidious forms of political exploitation is voter suppression. Through complex gerrymandering, restrictive voting laws, and the spread of misinformation about voting processes, certain groups deliberately disenfranchise segments of the population to maintain power. The complexity of these tactics ensures that most voters remain unaware of how their voting power is being manipulated.

However, all is not lost. We can fight back against this exploitation of ignorance through active resistance. Civic education, teaching critical thinking and media literacy, can equip citizens to recognize manipulation and demand accountability. Transparent governance, supported by whistleblowers and investigative journalism, plays a vital role in exposing corruption and misinformation.

Grassroots movements have shown the potential of informed, organized resistance. From civil rights campaigns to climate activism, these movements empower citizens to challenge political exploitation and demand policies that prioritize the common good.

The exploitation of ignorance is not inevitable. A well-informed electorate can hold leaders accountable, reject propaganda, and demand policies that benefit all of society. Reclaiming politics begins with reclaiming knowledge, seeking truth, embracing complexity, and rejecting the easy answers that ignorance offers.

As we move forward, it's crucial that we remain vigilant against the tactics of division and misinformation. Only by working together, across artificial divides, can we build a truly democratic society that serves all its citizens, not just those in power.

Chapter 13

The Ignorance-Fanaticism Feedback Loop

Ignorance and fanaticism is ever busy and needs feeding. - Clarence Darrow

In our increasingly complex and interconnected world, the relationship between ignorance and fanaticism has become a pressing concern. In 2013, the world watched in horror as the terrorist group ISIS systematically destroyed ancient artifacts in Mosul, Iraq, declaring them "idolatrous." This act of cultural erasure was not merely violence, it was fanaticism, rooted in a warped interpretation of history and religion. The perpetrators were not just armed extremists; they were individuals indoctrinated into a worldview that rejected nuance, evidence, and dialogue. Their actions exemplify a timeless truth: fanaticism thrives where ignorance prevails.

Ignorance creates fertile ground for fanaticism.

Whether religious, political, or ideological, fanaticism depends on the erosion of curiosity, the dismissal of opposing perspectives, and the glorification of simplistic narratives. Ignorance and fanaticism form a self-reinforcing cycle, one that has fueled humanity's darkest chapters and continues to threaten global stability today. By examining historical precedents, psychological mechanisms, and modern sociopolitical trends, we uncover how dismantling this cycle requires prioritizing education, critical thinking, and empathy. Fanaticism is marked by an uncompromising adherence to a cause, often accompanied by hostility toward dissent. Historian Eric Hoffer, in The True Believer, describes fanatics as individuals who "dread the present" and seek refuge in absolutist ideologies. Whether jihadist extremists or far-right militias, fanatics share a common trait: they view the world in binaries (us vs. them, sacred vs. profane) and see compromise as weakness.

Ignorance does not cause fanaticism but enables it. When people are deprived of education or taught to distrust expertise, they become vulnerable to manipulative narratives. Fanaticism, in turn, reinforces ignorance by demonizing curiosity.

Ignorance as a Catalyst for Extremism

History is littered with examples of ignorance and fanaticism intertwining to catastrophic effect.

The Crusades: Faith Over Reason

The medieval Crusades were justified through a deliberate distortion of religious doctrine. Pope Urban II's call to retake Jerusalem in 1095 relied on a populace largely illiterate and dependent on clerical authority. By framing Muslims as "enemies of Christ," the Church suppressed critical questions about the ethical implications of holy war. The result was centuries of violence fueled by willful ignorance.

Nazi Germany: The Cult of Pseudoscience

The Nazis exploited scientific illiteracy to propagate eugenics. By cherry-picking Darwinian concepts and promoting racist pseudoscience, they convinced millions that genocide was a biological necessity. Joseph Goebbels' propaganda machine thrived on a population uneducated in critical media literacy, illustrating how ignorance amplifies fanaticism.

The Salem Witch Trials: Fear of the Unknown

In 1692, the Puritan community of Salem executed 20 people for witchcraft. The trials emerged from a combination of superstition, religious dogmatism, and ignorance of natural phenomena (e.g., ergot poisoning causing "bewitchment" symptoms). The hysteria persisted because questioning the trials' legitimacy was equated with siding with the devil.

In each case, fanaticism was sustained by restricting access to education, stigmatizing dissent, and promoting fear of the "other."

The Psychology of Closed Minds

Cognitive science reveals why ignorance and fanaticism are mutually reinforcing. It sheds light on the psychological mechanisms that trap individuals in rigid belief systems.

Confirmation Bias

In the vast landscape of cognitive biases that shape human thinking, perhaps none is more insidious – or more dangerous – than confirmation bias.

This fundamental flaw in our reasoning doesn't just affect individual decision-making; it serves as the bedrock upon which fanaticism builds its unshakeable towers of certainty. Consider how confirmation bias operates: we naturally seek information that confirms our existing beliefs while dismissing or discounting evidence that challenges them. It's a comfortable mental shortcut that, in our ancestral past, might have served us well. Today, however, it acts as an accelerant for extremist thinking and ideological entrenchment.

The journey from reasonable belief to fanaticism often begins innocently enough. Someone develops an interest in a particular viewpoint or cause. Initially, they might approach it with genuine curiosity. But as they delve deeper, confirmation bias begins its subtle work. Each piece of supporting evidence is cataloged and celebrated, while contradictory information is rationalized away or ignored entirely.

The mind becomes an ever-more-efficient filtering system, separating "acceptable" information from "threatening" facts. What makes this process particularly dangerous is its self-reinforcing nature. As individuals become more invested in their beliefs, they tend to seek out like-minded people and information sources that mirror their viewpoints.

Social media algorithms, understanding this human tendency, helpfully serve up content that aligns with existing views. Each click, each share, each moment of engagement deepens the groove of conviction.

The transformation from belief to fanaticism occurs

when this filtering process becomes so advanced that contrary evidence isn't merely ignored – it's seen as active persecution. At this stage, challenges to one's beliefs are no longer treated as opportunities for discussion or learning, but as attacks that must be defended against. The fanatic's worldview becomes not just a set of beliefs, but a core part of their identity.

What makes confirmation bias particularly troubling in the modern era is how technology amplifies its effects. We no longer have to work hard to find information that confirms our beliefs – it finds us. Our digital worlds become perfectly curated echo chambers, where every piece of information serves to strengthen our existing convictions. The algorithms that power our online experiences understand that engagement often means agreement, and they're more than happy to provide it. The antidote to this cycle isn't simple, but it begins with awareness. Understanding that confirmation bias is not something that happens to "other people" – it's a fundamental aspect of human cognition that affects us all – is the first step.

The second is actively seeking out viewpoints that challenge our own, not to adopt them necessarily, but to understand them and to test our own convictions against their strongest counterarguments. Perhaps most importantly, we must learn to hold our beliefs more loosely. This doesn't mean abandoning conviction entirely, but rather maintaining a healthy skepticism about our own certainty. The most dangerous aspect of fanaticism isn't necessarily the beliefs themselves, but the unshakeable certainty with which they're held.

As we navigate an increasingly polarized world, our relationship with confirmation bias will help determine whether we contribute to further division or work toward understanding. The choice isn't between having strong beliefs and having no beliefs at all – it's between holding those beliefs with humility and wielding them as weapons of certainty. The path forward requires us to embrace discomfort, to actively seek out information that challenges our views, and to remember that the most dangerous lies are often the ones we tell ourselves. Only by acknowledging and actively working to counteract our confirmation bias can we hope to build bridges across the ideological chasms that increasingly define our world.

Cognitive Dissonance and Doublethink

In the landscape of human psychology, few phenomena are as fascinating and troubling as our ability to hold contradictory beliefs simultaneously. This cognitive feat, explored through both Festinger's theory of cognitive dissonance and Orwell's concept of doublethink, plays a crucial role in the development and maintenance of fanatical beliefs and behaviors.

When we encounter information that challenges our deeply held beliefs, we experience cognitive dissonance – a state of psychological discomfort that demands resolution. The human mind, rather than simply accepting new evidence and adjusting its worldview, often engages in elaborate mental contortions to preserve existing beliefs.

This is where doublethink enters the picture – the ability to simultaneously accept two contradictory beliefs as correct, particularly when one aligns with ideology and the other with observable reality. Consider the fanatic who proclaims absolute devotion to truth while willfully ignoring evidence that contradicts their beliefs. They might declare themselves champions of freedom while advocating for the suppression of dissenting voices, or preach compassion while justifying cruelty toward outsiders. These are not merely examples of hypocrisy – they represent a more complex psychological mechanism where both beliefs are held as true, despite their obvious contradiction.

The relationship between cognitive dissonance and fanaticism operates as a self-reinforcing cycle. When faced with contradictory evidence, the fanatic experiences intense cognitive dissonance. Rather than questioning their beliefs, they often double down, employing increasingly sophisticated forms of doublethink to maintain their worldview. This process can transform ordinary cognitive dissonance into a powerful engine of radicalization.

Several psychological mechanisms facilitate this process:

First, there's the phenomenon of belief perseverance – the tendency to cling to beliefs even after the evidence supporting them has been thoroughly debunked. This combines with confirmation bias, where individuals actively seek information that supports their existing beliefs while dismissing contradictory evidence.

Second, the social aspect of fanaticism provides a powerful support structure for doublethink. Within ideological bubbles, contradictory beliefs aren't just tolerated – they're often celebrated as profound insights. Fellow believers provide validation and ready-made rationalizations, making it easier to maintain cognitive dissonance without conscious discomfort.

Third, the emotional investment in fanatical beliefs creates a psychological stake too valuable to surrender. The more someone has sacrificed for their beliefs, the more motivated they become to preserve them, even in the face of glaring contradictions.

The consequences of this dynamic extend far beyond

individual psychology. When groups of people engage in collective doublethink, it can lead to the normalization of extreme positions and the justification of actions that would otherwise be considered unthinkable. Historical examples abound, from religious persecution to political purges, where societies employed doublethink to reconcile professed ideals with brutal realities.

Understanding these mechanisms is crucial for addressing fanaticism in its many forms. Simply presenting contrary evidence rarely helps – it often triggers defensive reactions that strengthen existing beliefs. Instead, effective intervention might require creating safe spaces for people to examine their own contradictions without feeling threatened. The path forward likely involves promoting intellectual humility and metacognition – the ability to think critically about one's own thought processes. By understanding how cognitive dissonance and doublethink operate in our own minds, we can better resist their ability to lead us down the path of fanaticism.

The interplay between cognitive dissonance and doublethink serves as a psychological engine for fanaticism, enabling individuals and groups to maintain increasingly extreme positions while believing themselves entirely rational and consistent. Breaking this cycle requires more than just counter-arguments – it demands a deeper understanding of human psychology and the development of tools to help people recognize and address their own cognitive contradictions.

The Role of Fear

Fear of the unknown drives both ignorance and fanaticism. Fear has long been recognized as a powerful force in human behavior, but its role in fueling fanaticism is particularly insidious and dangerous. Recent research and philosophical analyses have shed light on how fear intertwines with identity and sacred values to create a perfect storm for fanatical beliefs and actions. Studies show that individuals with lower educational attainment are more susceptible to fear-based propaganda. Extremist groups exploit this by framing themselves as protectors against imagined threats (e.g., "immigrants will destroy our culture").

At the core of fanaticism lies a perceived threat to one's identity and values. Fanatics experience fear on multiple levels. Fear of the out-group, fear of dissent within their own group, and even fear of their own inner doubts. This multifaceted fear creates a self-reinforcing cycle, where the fanatic becomes increasingly hostile to any form of opposition or questioning of their beliefs.

The digital age has exacerbated this problem by creating echo chambers that amplify fears and reinforce extreme viewpoints. Social media algorithms and online communities can quickly turn discordant views into full-blown fanaticism, with real-world consequences. The 2020 U.S. presidential election aftermath serves as a stark example of how fears about election integrity can spiral into violent fanaticism.

Perhaps most troubling is how fanaticism feeds on existential uncertainty. In a world of increasing complexity and rapid change, the absolutist certainty offered by fanatical ideologies can be alluring. Fanatics flee from the discomfort of ambiguity, seeking refuge in rigid beliefs and hostile antagonism towards dissenters.

To combat the rise of fanaticism, we must address its root causes. This includes fostering media literacy, promoting critical thinking skills, and creating spaces for respectful dialogue across ideological divides. Additionally, we need to reframe uncertainty not as a threat, but as an opportunity for growth and understanding.

Ultimately, the antidote to fear-driven fanaticism is not fearlessness, but courage. The courage to face complexity, embrace uncertainty, and engage with those who hold different views. Only by confronting our fears head-on can we hope to build a society resilient to the siren call of fanaticism.

Fanaticism, at its core, is the abandonment of reason in favor of absolute conviction. It thrives in environments where critical thinking is discouraged and nuanced understanding is eschewed. It is nurtured by ignorance, which provides a fertile ground of incomplete knowledge, misinformation, and emotional manipulation.

The partnership between the Cult of Ignorance and fanaticism poses a significant threat to reason, unity, and progress. However, just as ignorance feeds fanaticism, knowledge can dismantle it. By fostering a culture of critical thinking, empathy, and dialogue, we can break this dangerous cycle.

The choice lies before us: Will we allow ignorance to lead us into the darkness of fanaticism, or will we rise together toward the light of knowledge? As Vinton Cerf reminds us, embracing learning and education is not just a trend, but the key to our future. It is through this embrace that we can hope to break the ignorance-fanaticism feedback loop and build a more informed, compassionate, and rational society.

Chapter 14

The Commodification of Ignorance

*If you think education is expensive,
try ignorance. - Jeff Rich*

Ignorance is no longer merely a lack of knowledge. It has become a lucrative commodity. In the digital age, industries profit from spreading misinformation, sensationalism, and oversimplified narratives. Isaac Asimov's warning about the "cult of ignorance" is starkly relevant today, as ignorance is systematically packaged, sold, and weaponized.

This transformation of ignorance into a marketable product has profound implications for our society. The digital revolution, while providing unprecedented access to information, has paradoxically created an environment where misinformation thrives. Social media platforms and the internet have become the main arenas for what some experts call "neo-ignorance," where individuals, regardless of their education level, are often unaware of the limits of their knowledge.

A Historical Perspective

Throughout history, the exploitation of ignorance has proven to be a lucrative business model, evolving from patent medicines in the 19th century to today's digital misinformation ecosystem. This essay explores how ignorance has been systematically packaged, sold, and weaponized, tracing its development through key historical periods.

The 19th century saw the rise of patent medicines, unregulated concoctions sold with grandiose claims of curing various ailments. These products, despite their name, were not patented in the modern sense but relied on proprietary formulas marketed under catchy names. Examples like Dr. Williams' Pink Pills for Pale People and Cocaine Toothache Drops demonstrate how these products exploited societal anxieties and lack of medical knowledge.

Patent medicine advertisers employed tactics such as fear-based marketing and celebrity endorsements to sell their products. The impact of this industry was significant, leading to public health crises and eventually prompting the Pure Food and Drug Act of 1906, the first U.S. law regulating consumer products.

The late 19th and early 20th centuries saw the rise of yellow journalism, exemplified by the rivalry between Joseph Pulitzer's New York World and William Randolph Hearst's New York Journal. These newspapers prioritized sensationalism over accuracy, shaping public opinion through emotionally charged narratives. The Spanish-American War of 1898 is a prime example of how yellow journalism could influence real-world events.

The 20th century witnessed the tobacco industry's pioneering strategies to manufacture doubt about scientific consensus. Internal documents from tobacco companies reveal deliberate efforts to create uncertainty about the health risks of smoking. These tactics delayed public awareness of smoking's dangers for decades.

The fossil fuel industry later adopted similar strategies to combat climate science. Companies like ExxonMobil, despite internal knowledge of climate risks, funded denial groups to cast doubt on scientific findings. This delayed global climate action by decades, contributing to today's accelerating environmental crises.

The digital revolution has transformed ignorance into a scalable, profitable commodity. The rise of clickbait content and social media algorithms that prioritize engagement over accuracy has created an environment where misinformation spreads rapidly. Platforms like Facebook and YouTube have been criticized for algorithms that push users towards extreme content to maximize engagement.

Throughout these historical periods, the commodification of ignorance has followed a recurring pattern: exploiting cognitive biases, monetizing emotion, and delaying accountability. From patent medicines to climate denial, industries have prioritized profit over truth, often stalling regulation until crises erupt.

The legacy of these historical precedents is evident in today's "post-truth" era, where misinformation spreads faster than ever before. The lessons from history are clear: without systemic checks, ignorance will always be a profitable and dangerous commodity. As we navigate the complex information landscape of the 21st century, understanding this historical context is crucial for developing effective strategies to combat the ongoing commodification of ignorance.

The Role of Media and Entertainment in the Commodification of Ignorance

In today's digital age, modern media ecosystems have evolved to thrive on ignorance, leveraging emotional triggers to capture attention and generate revenue. This transformation has profound implications for the quality of information we consume and the way we understand the world around us.

Clickbait Journalism: The Rise of Shallow Content

One of the most visible manifestations of this trend is the proliferation of clickbait journalism. Clickbait headlines, designed to entice users into clicking, have become a dominant form of online media. A study conducted in 2024 found that clickbait headlines can evoke users' arousal and curiosity, often at the expense of journalistic quality.

The success of platforms like BuzzFeed in the early 2010s, with their listicles and quizzes, set a precedent for prioritizing shareability over substance. This trend has normalized shallow content across the media landscape. As traditional newspapers struggle to survive, partisan outlets have filled the void with hyper-sensationalized content, further eroding the quality of public discourse.

The impact of clickbait extends beyond mere annoyance. Research suggests that while clickbait headlines may increase user engagement in the short term, they have a broadly negative impact on audience perceptions of journalistic credibility and quality. This erosion of trust in media sources has far-reaching consequences for public understanding of complex issues and the functioning of democratic societies.

Reality TV and Infotainment: Blurring the Lines

The rise of reality TV and infotainment has further blurred the lines between entertainment and information. Shows like "The Kardashians" have glorified fame over expertise, reinforcing the idea that visibility equals authority. This trend has serious implications for how we perceive and value knowledge in society.

Reality TV's influence extends beyond mere entertainment. Studies have found that reality shows can exacerbate body anxiety, increase physical aggression, and distort viewers' expectations for romantic relationships. For young viewers in particular, these shows can present culturally constructed norms of gender, race, class, and sexuality as "natural," potentially shaping their worldviews in problematic ways.

The impact of reality TV on teens is particularly concerning. These shows often promote materialism, excessive partying, and inappropriate behavior within peer groups. They frequently feature interpersonal drama, aggression, and bullying, potentially normalizing these behaviors for young viewers. The long-term effects of this exposure on societal values and interpersonal relationships are only beginning to be understood.

Conspiracy Entertainment: Monetizing Fringe Ideas

Perhaps the most insidious trend in the commodification of ignorance is the rise of conspiracy entertainment. Podcasts like The Joe Rogan Experience have platformed conspiracy theorists, monetizing fringe ideas through ad revenue and subscriptions. This trend has accelerated the spread of misinformation and pseudoscience, with real-world consequences for public health and democratic discourse.

Even well-intentioned media can inadvertently contribute to this problem. Documentaries like Netflix's "The Social Dilemma," while critiquing tech's exploitation of ignorance, themselves simplify complex issues for viral appeal. This highlights the challenge of addressing these issues within the current media ecosystem, where even critical voices are subject to the same pressures of engagement and virality.

The Broader Impact

The cumulative effect of these trends is a media landscape that often prioritizes engagement over accuracy, emotion over reason, and simplification over nuance. This has significant implications for public understanding of complex issues like climate change, public health, and democratic processes. Research has shown that the abundance of information available, especially on social media, can give users the illusion of knowing – a mismatch between what users think they know and what they actually comprehend. This phenomenon, combined with the tendency of users to not read entire articles or verify sources, creates a perfect storm for the spread of misinformation and the entrenchment of ignorance.

Moreover, the algorithmic nature of social media platforms tends to create echo chambers, where users are primarily exposed to information that aligns with their existing beliefs. This can reinforce simplistic narratives and make it harder for more nuanced perspectives to gain traction.

The commodification of ignorance in media and

entertainment presents a significant challenge to our society. It undermines the quality of public discourse, erodes trust in institutions, and potentially threatens the foundations of democratic decision-making.

Addressing this issue will require a multifaceted approach. Media literacy education must be prioritized to equip individuals with the skills to critically evaluate the information they encounter. Responsible journalism that prioritizes accuracy and depth over sensationalism must be supported and encouraged. And perhaps most importantly, we as consumers must demand better, recognizing that our attention and engagement are valuable commodities that should not be given away lightly.

The Advertising Industry: Selling Falsehoods

In today's digital age, the advertising industry has undergone a significant transformation, evolving from simply promoting products to selling ideologies. This shift has often involved exploiting cognitive biases and leveraging sophisticated psychological tactics to influence consumer behavior. As we examine this trend, it becomes clear that the line between marketing and manipulation has become increasingly blurred.

Pseudoscience in Marketing

One of the most concerning trends in modern advertising is the proliferation of pseudoscience in marketing campaigns. Companies and influencers alike have capitalized on the public's desire for quick fixes and miracle cures, often using scientific-sounding jargon to lend credibility to dubious claims.

A prime example of this is the rise of "wellness"

brands that promote products with little to no scientific backing. These companies often use vague terms like "clinically proven" or "all-natural" without providing concrete evidence to support their claims. This tactic preys on consumers' scientific illiteracy and their desire for simple solutions to complex health issues.

Social media has amplified this problem, with influencers promoting unproven supplements and weight loss products to their followers. These promotions often rely on aspirational imagery and personal testimonials rather than scientific evidence, making it difficult for consumers to distinguish between genuine health advice and marketing ploys.

Fear-Based Advertising

Another concerning trend in advertising is the use of fear to motivate consumer behavior. This tactic has been particularly prevalent in pharmaceutical advertising and political campaigns. In the United States, direct-to-consumer drug advertisements have been criticized for exaggerating benefits while downplaying risks. These ads often encourage self-diagnosis and can lead to unnecessary medication use.

The use of fear in these advertisements can be particularly problematic, as it may lead consumers to make health decisions based on emotion rather than medical necessity.

Political advertising has also increasingly relied on fear-based tactics. Campaigns often use threatening scenarios to scare voters into supporting particular candidates or policies. This approach not only manipulates voters' emotions but can also contribute to a more polarized and anxious society.

Data-Driven Manipulation

The rise of big data and advanced analytics has given advertisers unprecedented ability to target and influence consumers. While this can lead to more personalized and relevant advertising, it also opens the door for manipulation on a massive scale.

The Cambridge Analytica scandal in 2016 highlighted the potential for abuse in data-driven advertising. By harvesting personal data from millions of Facebook users, the company was able to create highly targeted political advertisements designed to influence voting behavior. This incident raised serious concerns about privacy and the potential for data-driven manipulation in democratic processes.

The Impact on Society

The cumulative effect of these advertising practices is significant. They contribute to the spread of misinformation, erode trust in institutions, and can have real impacts on public health and democratic processes. Research has shown that when advertisements appear alongside misinformation, it can increase the credibility of the false information. This creates a dangerous feedback loop, incentivising the creation of more misleading content and further eroding public trust in media and advertising.

Moreover, the prevalence of fear-based and pseudo-scientific advertising can have tangible impacts on public health. A recent study found that fear appeals in vaccination advertising can actually be less effective in promoting vaccination intentions, particularly among adult populations in Western cultures.

As we navigate an increasingly complex media

landscape, it's crucial that we remain vigilant consumers of information. The advertising industry's shift towards selling ideologies rather than products presents significant challenges for society.

To combat these trends, we need stronger regulations on advertising claims, particularly in areas that impact public health and democratic processes. Additionally, there's a pressing need for improved media literacy education to help consumers critically evaluate the messages they encounter.

Ultimately, the responsibility lies not just with regulators and educators, but with advertisers themselves. Ethical advertising practices that prioritize truth and transparency over manipulation are not just morally right – they're essential for maintaining consumer trust in the long term. It is crucial that we demand better from the advertising industry.

Only by holding advertisers accountable and fostering a more discerning consumer base can we hope to create a media ecosystem that informs rather than misleads, and empowers rather than exploits.

The Consequences of Commodifying Ignorance

The commodification of ignorance has become a pressing issue in our modern society, with far-reaching consequences that affect various aspects of our lives. This essay explores the societal, economic, and democratic costs of this troubling trend.

Societal Costs

One of the most significant impacts of commodified ignorance is the erosion of trust in institutions and information sources. A 2019 study by Pew Research

Center revealed that 64% of Americans believe fake news causes "a great deal of confusion" about basic facts. This widespread distrust has far-reaching implications for social cohesion and our ability to address complex challenges collectively. The COVID-19 pandemic starkly illustrated the public health consequences of misinformation. Vaccine hesitancy, fueled by the spread of false information, prolonged the pandemic and overwhelmed healthcare systems. The commodification of ignorance in this context led to tangible harm, with increased hospitalizations and deaths that could have been prevented with accurate information and trust in scientific expertise.

Economic Costs

The economic impact of commodified ignorance is equally concerning. Climate change denial, a prime example of weaponized ignorance, has led to delayed action on crucial environmental policies. According to recent estimates, this inaction could cost the global economy $23 trillion annually by 2050. The persistence of climate change denial, often fueled by industries with vested interests in maintaining the status quo, demonstrates how the commodification of ignorance can have severe long-term economic consequences.

The cryptocurrency market provides another example of how commodified ignorance can lead to significant financial losses. Influencer-driven hype and misinformation contributed to the collapse of platforms like FTX in 2022, wiping out an estimated $2 trillion in market value. This incident highlights how the spread of unreliable information, often motivated by profit, can lead to widespread economic harm.

Democratic Erosion

Perhaps most alarmingly, the commodification of ignorance poses a direct threat to democratic institutions. The 2016 U.S. election interference by Russia's Internet Research Agency (IRA) demonstrated how foreign actors could exploit social divisions and spread misinformation through targeted advertising on platforms like Facebook. This incident revealed the vulnerability of democratic processes to manipulation through the strategic use of misinformation.

The authoritarian playbook of leaders like Hungary's Viktor Orbán further illustrates how the commodification of ignorance can be used to consolidate power. By controlling state media and spreading disinformation, such leaders can manipulate public opinion and undermine democratic norms. This trend is not limited to Hungary; similar tactics have been observed in various countries, raising concerns about the global state of democracy.

The commodification of ignorance represents a significant challenge to our society, with consequences that extend far beyond individual misinformation. It erodes trust, threatens public health, hampers economic progress, and undermines democratic institutions. Addressing this issue requires a multifaceted approach, including improved media literacy education, stronger regulations on the spread of misinformation, and a renewed commitment to evidence-based decision-making at all levels of society.

We need to recognize the value of knowledge and expertise, and work to create systems that prioritize truth over profit. Only by actively resisting the commodification of ignorance can we hope to build a more informed, prosperous, and democratic society.

Chapter 15

Reclaiming Rational Discourse

I know nothing, except the fact of my ignorance.
- Diogenes

The world today feels like a battleground of opposing viewpoints, exacerbated by echo chambers and weaponised by inflammatory speech. Rational discourse, which is the bedrock of democracy and progress, has been sidelined in favour of sensationalism and tribal loyalties. But while the current state of public conversation may feel disheartening, all is not lost. This chapter examines the barriers to rational discourse and offers practical strategies for reclaiming it in a polarized world.

The Collapse of Civil Dialogue

In an era where information flows at unprecedented speeds and platforms for expression multiply daily, we find ourselves paradoxically less capable of meaningful dialogue than ever before. The collapse of civil discourse represents not just a failure of communication, but a fundamental threat to the very foundations of democratic society.

The art of disagreement – once considered a cornerstone of intellectual growth – has devolved into a gladiatorial spectacle where the goal is not understanding, but victory at any cost. We've replaced the patient work of reasoning with the immediate gratification of rhetorical body slams, trading the seminar room for the boxing ring. What makes this transformation particularly insidious is how it masquerades as progress.

We convince ourselves that our inability to engage with opposing viewpoints represents moral clarity rather than intellectual poverty. Each blocked account, each dismissed argument, each demonized opponent becomes another brick in the walls we build around our minds. The technological architecture of our digital town square bears significant responsibility. Social media algorithms, designed to maximize engagement, inadvertently reward the most inflammatory voices while burying measured responses. We've created an attention economy where thoughtful analysis can't compete with the dopamine hit of righteous outrage. But technology alone doesn't explain our predicament.

We've witnessed a broader cultural shift where the very concept of objective truth has become suspect. In this new paradigm, personal experience trumps empirical evidence, and feelings carry more weight than facts. This isn't to dismiss the importance of lived experience, but rather to recognize that when subjective perception becomes the only accepted currency of debate, we lose our shared basis for discussion.

Perhaps most troubling is how this deterioration of

discourse has infected our institutions of learning. Universities, once bastions of intellectual exploration, increasingly resemble echo chambers where challenging ideas are viewed as threats rather than opportunities for growth. Students arrive and depart without ever having their core beliefs seriously challenged – a developmental tragedy masked as ideological protection.

The path forward requires more than just lamenting our current state. We need to actively rebuild the infrastructure of rational discourse. This means creating spaces – both physical and digital – where good-faith disagreement is not just tolerated but celebrated. It means developing educational approaches that teach students not just what to think, but how to think, and most importantly, how to be wrong gracefully.

We must also recognize that civil dialogue isn't just about politeness – it's about intellectual humility. The ability to say "I might be mistaken" represents not weakness, but the highest form of cognitive sophistication. This humility, paired with rigorous critical thinking, forms the foundation of genuine intellectual progress.

The collapse of civil dialogue isn't inevitable. But its revival will require us to choose the harder path – to resist the allure of rhetorical violence, to engage with ideas we find uncomfortable, and to recognize that those who disagree with us aren't necessarily our enemies. In short, we must learn again what our predecessors knew: that civilization itself rests upon our ability to disagree productively.

The stakes could not be higher. In a world facing unprecedented challenges – from climate change to artificial intelligence – we cannot afford to abandon the tools of rational discourse. Our survival may well depend on our ability to restore the art of civil dialogue, not as a luxury of polite society, but as an essential mechanism for human progress.

The Polarization Problem

When future historians examine the early decades of the 21st century, they may well identify our growing ideological segregation as one of the defining challenges of our time. Like water naturally flowing into separate channels, we have gradually carved ourselves into distinct tribes, each with its own media ecosystem, social networks, and version of reality.

This self-sorting goes far beyond traditional political divisions. We now choose our neighborhoods, schools, entertainment, and even grocery stores based on perceived ideological alignment. The barista who serves our morning coffee, the gym where we exercise, the restaurants we frequent – all have become unwitting signals of tribal affiliation. We've transformed consumer choices into identity markers, turning even the most mundane decisions into statements of political allegiance.

The architects of this division – politicians, media figures, and social media influencers – have discovered a profitable truth: division sells better than unity. Outrage generates more clicks than understanding, and fear drives higher engagement than hope. They've weaponized our tribal instincts, transforming natural human tendencies toward group identity into tools for manipulation and profit.

Social media platforms, despite their promise of connecting humanity, have instead become sophisticated sorting machines. Their algorithms, designed to maximize engagement, feed us an endless stream of content that confirms our existing beliefs while systematically filtering out challenging perspectives. We don't just create echo chambers – we pay tech companies to build them for us, brick by digital brick.

The consequences extend far beyond our screens. In workplaces, families, and communities, we increasingly view those with different political views as not just wrong, but morally deficient or intellectually compromised. This assumption of bad faith makes genuine dialogue nearly impossible. How can you have a productive conversation with someone you've pre-judged as evil or stupid?

Politicians have mastered the art of exploiting these divisions. Rather than seeking broad coalitions or common ground, many have found it more expedient to energize their base through demonization of the "other side." The result is a political system that rewards extremism and punishes moderation, pushing our representatives toward increasingly radical positions to maintain their support.

Traditional media, facing intense competition for attention, has largely abandoned its role as a neutral arbiter of facts. Instead, news outlets increasingly cater to specific ideological audiences, providing them not just with information, but with ready-made narratives that confirm their worldview. The business model of journalism has shifted from informing the public to validating their preexisting beliefs.

The most insidious aspect of this polarization is how it becomes self-reinforcing. Each act of ideological self-sorting makes the next one easier to justify. Every time we disengage from those who think differently, we make it harder to bridge the gap in the future. We're creating social muscle memory for division.

Yet there's hope in understanding this dynamic. The very fact that polarization is largely manufactured – a product of deliberate choices and perverse incentives –

suggests it can be unmade through equally deliberate choices. We can choose to seek out diverse perspectives, to engage with those who think differently, to resist the comfortable pull of ideological segregation. This isn't about compromising our values or accepting every viewpoint as equally valid. Rather, it's about recognizing that our current trajectory toward ever-greater polarization threatens the very foundations of democratic society.

A democracy requires citizens capable of seeing each other as fellow humans worthy of respect and engagement, even in disagreement. The path forward requires both individual and systemic changes. As individuals, we must actively resist the urge to self-segregate and challenge ourselves to engage with different perspectives. Systemically, we need to redesign our digital spaces and reform our political institutions to reward bridge-building rather than division.

The choice before us is clear: we can continue down the path of increasing polarization, allowing ourselves to be sorted into ever-more-hostile tribes, or we can actively work to rebuild the social and institutional bridges that make democracy possible. The future of our civic life hangs in the balance.

The Death of Shared Reality

Remember when we could agree on what happened yesterday? It seems almost quaint now, like reminiscing about rotary phones or card catalogs. We find ourselves in an unprecedented moment where the very concept of objective reality has become contested territory, where "fact-checking" is dismissed as partisan warfare, and where the phrase "do your own research" has become a battle cry for those rejecting traditional sources of knowledge.

The erosion of our shared reality didn't happen overnight. Like a slow-moving landslide, it began with subtle shifts: the proliferation of cable news channels, the rise of talk radio, the dawn of the internet. Each technological advance promised to democratize information but instead balkanised it, creating increasingly specialised channels of reality customised to our preferences and prejudices.

Social media algorithms accelerated this splintering, creating personalized reality tunnels that feed us information confirming our existing beliefs while screening out contradictory evidence. We no longer simply disagree about solutions – we disagree about what problems exist in the first place. Climate change, election results, public health measures – these aren't just points of policy debate anymore, but fundamentally different versions of reality.

The traditional gatekeepers of information – newspapers, universities, scientific institutions – haven't just lost their monopoly on truth; they've lost their ability to serve as shared reference points for society. In their place, we've seen the rise of alternative information ecosystems, each with its own experts, evidence, and epistemological frameworks.

It's no longer enough to fact-check a claim; we must now debate what constitutes a fact in the first place. This fragmentation of reality has profound implications for democracy. How can citizens make informed decisions when they can't agree on basic facts? How can we solve complex societal problems when we can't even agree on their existence? The marketplace of ideas assumes that truth will eventually prevail, but what happens when the very concept of truth becomes relative?

The role of technology in this transformation cannot

be overstated. Artificial intelligence and deepfake technology have made it increasingly difficult to distinguish authentic content from sophisticated fabrications. Social media platforms, optimized for engagement rather than accuracy, have created an attention economy where sensational falsehoods consistently outperform nuanced truths.

Perhaps most troubling is how this splintering of reality has become self-reinforcing. Each time we retreat into our preferred information bubbles, our worldview becomes more resistant to contrary evidence. We develop intellectual antibodies against information that challenges our beliefs, dismissing it as fake news or disinformation before we even process its content.

The psychological comfort of these reality bubbles is undeniable. It's reassuring to have every belief confirmed, every prejudice validated, every complex problem reduced to simple narratives of good versus evil. But this comfort comes at a devastating cost to our collective ability to understand and address real-world challenges.

The path forward requires more than just better fact-checking or media literacy. We need to rebuild the social infrastructure that once allowed us to negotiate shared understandings of reality. This means creating spaces where different worldviews can meaningfully interact, developing new models of trust and verification, and finding ways to make truth more compelling than comfortable fiction.

We must also confront an uncomfortable question: Is a shared reality even possible in a world of algorithmic personalisation and infinite information choice? Perhaps the goal isn't to return to a single, monolithic truth, but to develop better ways of navigating between different versions of reality while maintaining our ability to act collectively when necessary.

The stakes could not be higher. Without some basic shared understanding of reality, democracy becomes impossible, replaced by competing tribes each living in their own bespoke version of truth. The great challenges of our time – climate change, technological disruption, global inequality – require collective action based on shared understanding. Without this foundation, we risk paralysis in the face of existential threats.

The death of shared reality isn't just an intellectual crisis – it's a practical one. Our ability to survive and thrive as a species has always depended on our capacity to build shared understandings of the world. Rebuilding this capacity may be the defining challenge of our age. The alternative is a world where truth becomes purely personal, and reality itself becomes optional – a world where we can no longer solve problems because we can no longer agree they exist.

The Price We Pay for Silence

We stand at a precipice, though many fail to recognize it. The breakdown of rational discourse in our society isn't just an abstract concern for academics or philosophers – it represents an existential threat to the foundations of civilization itself. As our ability to engage in reasoned debate crumbles, we're witnessing a cascade of consequences that threatens to reshape society in ways we can barely imagine.

Consider first the dissolution of trust, that invisible thread that binds societies together. When rational discourse fails, we lose more than just the ability to disagree productively – we lose the very mechanisms that allow us to build and maintain trust. In a world where every expert is suspected of hidden agendas, where every institution is presumed corrupt, and where every neighbor with a different viewpoint is seen as an enemy, the social fabric begins to unravel.

This erosion of trust creates a vacuum quickly filled by conspiracy theories and extremist ideologies. Without the guardrails of rational discourse, people become susceptible to manipulation by those who traffic in fear and outrage. The irony is bitter: in rejecting traditional sources of authority, many fall prey to far more insidious forms of influence.

Perhaps nowhere is the cost of this breakdown more evident than in our inability to address pressing societal challenges. Climate change looms as an existential threat, yet meaningful action remains paralyzed by our inability to engage in productive dialogue. Healthcare systems creak under mounting pressures while debate devolves into shouting matches. Income inequality widens while discussion of solutions becomes trapped in ideological warfare.

These aren't just policy debates gone awry – they represent fundamental failures of our collective problem-solving capacity. Complex challenges require nuanced solutions, careful consideration of trade-offs, and the ability to forge compromise. When rational discourse breaks down, we lose access to these essential tools of civilization.

The escalation from disagreement to conflict follows a predictable but devastating pattern. Without the release valve of meaningful dialogue, tensions build. Political differences transform into personal animosities. Policy debates become proxy battles in a broader cultural war. Each side becomes increasingly convinced that force – whether social, economic, or physical – is the only remaining option.

This progression from debate to violence isn't merely theoretical. History provides ample evidence of societies that, having lost the ability to resolve differences through dialogue, descended into conflict. Today's social media platforms offer perfect petri dishes for observing this process in real-time, as reasonable disagreements rapidly escalate into calls for action against the "other side."

The psychological toll of this breakdown cannot be overlooked. Living in a state of constant antagonism, where every interaction carries the potential for conflict, exacts a heavy price on mental health. The stress of navigating a world where rational discourse has broken down contributes to rising rates of anxiety and depression, creating a feedback loop that further impairs our collective ability to engage in meaningful dialogue.

What makes this crisis particularly insidious is its self-reinforcing nature. Each breakdown in communication makes the next one more likely. Each retreat from rational discourse makes future engagement more difficult. Each escalation to conflict makes peaceful resolution seem more distant. We risk entering a spiral from which recovery becomes increasingly difficult.

Yet understanding these dynamics also points toward potential solutions. If the breakdown of rational discourse represents a learned behavior, we can work to unlearn it. This requires deliberate effort at multiple levels: educational systems that teach critical thinking and civil debate, media platforms designed to reward substantive discussion rather than conflict, and cultural norms that celebrate intellectual humility and good-faith engagement.

The stakes could not be higher. Without the ability to engage in rational discourse, democracy itself becomes unsustainable. The complex challenges facing humanity – from artificial intelligence to genetic engineering to climate change – require unprecedented levels of cooperation and careful deliberation. Our survival may well depend on our ability to restore the art of rational discourse.

The path forward demands more than just lamenting what we've lost. It requires active commitment to rebuilding the infrastructure of rational discourse: creating safe spaces for difficult conversations, developing new tools for collaborative problem-solving, and cultivating the skills needed for productive disagreement. Most importantly, it requires each of us to resist the pull of antagonism and commit to the harder work of genuine dialogue.

The alternative – a world where might makes right and where complex problems remain perpetually unsolved – should motivate us to act before it's too late. The future of civilization may well depend on our ability to rediscover the art of rational discourse, not as a luxury, but as a fundamental survival skill for the challenges ahead.

Model Rational Discourse

Change begins at the individual level. We should demonstrate the principles of rational discourse. This includes active listening, asking clarifying questions, and acknowledging valid points even in opposing arguments. Public figures, educators, and influencers can play a vital role by modeling respectful dialogue in their own interactions.

The Art of Asking Questions: Why Socrates Still Matters

In an age of hot takes and gotcha moments, we might find salvation in the methods of a barefoot philosopher who walked the streets of Athens 2,400 years ago. The

Socratic method – that careful, questioning approach to understanding – offers more than just a historical curiosity. It provides a roadmap for rebuilding meaningful dialogue in our fractured world.

The genius of Socratic questioning lies not in its complexity but in its simplicity. By asking genuine, probing questions rather than making declarative statements, we create space for exploration rather than confrontation. This subtle shift transforms discussions from battles to be won into journeys to be shared.

When someone feels heard rather than attacked, the walls of defensive thinking begin to lower. Consider how different our current political discussions might look if we approached them with Socratic curiosity. Instead of declaring "Your position on immigration is wrong," we might ask "What experiences shaped your views on immigration?" Rather than dismissing someone's economic beliefs, we might inquire "How do you think that policy would affect different communities?" The shift from assertion to inquiry changes everything.

The Socratic emphasis on clarity serves as an antidote to the vague generalizations that often poison modern discourse. When we ask people to define their terms, explain their reasoning, and examine their assumptions, we're not just being pedantic – we're creating the conditions for genuine understanding. Vagueness is often where prejudice and logical fallacies hide; clarity is where genuine thinking begins.

The method's power lies in its ability to lead people to their own discoveries. When someone reaches a conclusion through their own reasoning, that understanding becomes part of their intellectual DNA in a way that external arguments never could. This is why Socrates saw himself as a midwife to ideas rather than a lecturer – he helped people give birth to their own insights.

Modern practitioners of Socratic dialogue, particularly in the street epistemology movement, have demonstrated its continued relevance. By engaging strangers in respectful conversations about their deeply held beliefs, these modern Socratics show how genuine curiosity can bridge seemingly insurmountable divides. Their success suggests that people aren't as closed-minded as we often assume – they just need the right conversational environment to explore their thoughts.

The method's focus on self-reflection offers a particularly valuable tool for our polarized times. In an era where certainty is often prized over curiosity, the Socratic approach reminds us that questioning our own beliefs is a sign of strength, not weakness. When we model this kind of intellectual humility, we create permission for others to do the same.

However, practicing the Socratic method requires more than just asking questions – it demands a fundamental shift in how we approach conversation. It requires genuine curiosity about others' perspectives, patience with the meandering nature of authentic dialogue, and the humility to admit that we might not have all the answers. In short, it requires us to be more interested in understanding than in winning.

The challenges to implementing this approach in our modern context are significant. Social media's rapid-fire nature doesn't easily accommodate the slow, deliberate pace of Socratic dialogue. Our political culture rewards certainty over curiosity, and our education system often prioritizes answers over questions. Yet these challenges make the method more necessary, not less.

Perhaps most importantly, the Socratic method offers a way to disagree without dehumanizing. In our current climate, where disagreement often leads to demonisation, this ability to explore differences while maintaining respect becomes crucial. When we engage others through questioning rather than attacking, we preserve the possibility of connection even across deep divides.

The method also provides a powerful tool for addressing misinformation and conspiracy theories. Rather than directly confronting false beliefs – which often leads to backfire effects – Socratic questioning can help people examine their own reasoning and sources of information. This gentle but persistent inquiry often proves more effective than direct debate.

As we face increasingly complex challenges as a society, the need for better methods of dialogue becomes more urgent. The Socratic method offers not just a philosophical approach but a practical tool for navigating disagreement, exploring complex issues, and building understanding across divides. In a world desperate for better conversation, this ancient wisdom might offer exactly what we need.

The question before us isn't whether to embrace Socratic dialogue, but how to adapt its timeless principles to modern challenges. In doing so, we might find that the path to better discourse doesn't require new technology or complicated systems – it simply requires us to remember how to ask good questions and listen carefully to the answers.

Political Reform: Money Talks, Democracy Whispers

The degradation of political discourse in our democracy isn't an accident – it's the predictable result of a system that values spectacle over substance and donor satisfaction over public service. While we bemoan the quality of our political debates, we rarely confront the underlying structures that make meaningful dialogue nearly impossible.

Campaign finance, far from being a mere technical issue, sits at the heart of our democratic dysfunction. When candidates must raise astronomical sums to remain competitive, their messages inevitably become shaped by the preferences of donors rather than the needs of voters. This financial pressure creates a perverse incentive structure where thoughtful policy discussions take a back seat to inflammatory rhetoric designed to drive donations.

The impact on political discourse is profound. Complex issues that demand nuanced discussion – healthcare, climate change, economic policy – get reduced to bumper-sticker slogans and attack ads. Politicians learn that raising money requires maintaining constant outrage, turning every issue into a crisis and every opponent into an enemy. The result is a political culture that rewards extremism and punishes moderation.

Our current debate formats compound these problems. The standard political debate has become a choreographed exercise in message delivery, where candidates recite pre-packaged talking points while trying to land "viral moments" that will play well on social media. These formats serve neither the candidates nor the voters, creating artificial constraints that make genuine discussion impossible.

The path to reform requires addressing both the financial and structural elements that shape political discourse. On the campaign finance front, we need comprehensive reforms that reduce candidates' dependence on large donors and dark money. This means strengthening disclosure requirements, closing loopholes that allow anonymous political spending, and exploring public financing options that could free candidates from the endless fundraising treadmill.

But financial reform alone isn't enough. We need to re-imagine how political debates function. Rather than ninety-second soundbites and gotcha questions, debates should provide candidates with the time and space to explain complex policies and engage in genuine dialogue. This might mean longer format discussions, topic-specific debates, or innovative formats that encourage substantive engagement rather than performative conflict.

Technology offers both challenges and opportunities in this transformation. While social media has often exacerbated the problems of shallow political discourse, it also provides platforms for deeper engagement. Imagine debates where candidates can share detailed policy proposals in real-time, or where voters can pose follow-up questions that demand specific answers rather than vague platitudes.

The role of media organizations in this reform cannot be overlooked. Current coverage often focuses on horse-race journalism and conflict, treating politics as sport rather than governance. Media outlets must resist the temptation to prioritize entertainment over information, even if that means sacrificing short-term ratings for long-term democratic health. Voters, too, must demand better.

As long as we reward politicians who traffic in oversimplification and demonisation, we'll continue to get exactly that. This means developing our own capacity for nuanced political thinking and supporting candidates who demonstrate genuine engagement with complex issues, even when their messages don't fit neatly into tweets or sound bites.

Education plays a crucial role in this transformation. Schools must better prepare citizens to engage with political issues critically and thoughtfully. This means teaching not just civic knowledge but also media literacy, critical thinking, and the ability to evaluate complex policy proposals.

The stakes in this reform effort couldn't be higher. In an era of unprecedented challenges – from climate change to artificial intelligence to global economic transformation – we cannot afford a political system that reduces every issue to its lowest common denominator. Our survival may depend on our ability to engage in sophisticated political dialogue about complex issues.

The question isn't whether we need political reform – it's whether we have the collective will to implement it. The current system serves powerful interests who benefit from shallow discourse and polarization. Change will require sustained effort from voters, activists, and reform-minded politicians willing to challenge the status quo.

The future of democracy depends on our ability to restore substance to political discourse. This means creating systems that reward thoughtful engagement over inflammatory rhetoric, that prioritize voter understanding over donor satisfaction, and that create space for the kind of detailed policy discussions our challenges demand. The alternative is a continued descent into political theater that entertains but fails to govern.

Community Programs:

Invest in programs that bring people from different backgrounds together to address shared challenges, fostering understanding and collaboration. Community programs that bring diverse groups together to tackle shared challenges are more vital than ever. These initiatives not only address pressing local issues but also serve as powerful catalysts for fostering understanding, empathy, and collaboration across societal divides.

One of the most significant benefits of such programs is their ability to break down the invisible barriers that often separate different segments of our communities. By bringing people from various backgrounds together—whether they differ in age, ethnicity, socioeconomic status, or political beliefs—these initiatives create opportunities for meaningful interaction that might not otherwise occur in our daily lives.

When diverse groups come together to address shared challenges, they quickly discover that what unites them is far more powerful than what divides them. Whether it's tackling environmental issues, improving local education, or addressing food insecurity, these common goals provide a foundation for cooperation and mutual understanding.

The impact of these community programs extends far beyond the immediate goals they set out to achieve. Participants often report a shift in their perspectives, a broadening of their worldviews, and a deeper appreciation for the experiences of others. This ripple effect can transform entire communities, gradually eroding stereotypes and prejudices that may have existed for generations.

Allocating resources to these programs is not just a feel-good measure; it's an investment in the social fabric of our society. By fostering collaboration and understanding at the grassroots level, we build more resilient, cohesive communities that are better equipped to face future challenges together.

A Future Worth Fighting For

Reclaiming rational discourse is not just an intellectual exercise. It is a moral imperative. Without it, societies will continue to fracture, misinformation will thrive, and progress will stagnate. But with it, humanity can move closer to solving its greatest challenges, from climate change to inequality to global conflict. By committing to truth, humility, and empathy, we can restore the art of conversation and rebuild the bridges that ignorance has torn down. Rational discourse is not just a skill; it is the foundation of a better, more just world.

In the end, the battle against ignorance is not just a fight for knowledge. It is a struggle for the very soul of our society. The future of our communities, our nations, and our planet, depends on the choices we make today. The cult of ignorance may be pervasive, but it is not invincible. Together, we can build a world where wisdom triumphs, where reason prevails, and where the pursuit of truth is celebrated as our highest calling.

Acknowledgments

I've lived through some of the most darkest periods of my life in the past few years. Writing this book has been a journey through shadows and light.

To my family: Mom and Dad, your quiet strength and boundless love have been my foundation. Your unwaivering belief in me, even when I faltered, was a lifeline. Through every crisis, every sleepless night, you reminded me that even the darkest storms pass. To my siblings, thank you for refusing to let me drown in the gloom.

And to my cousin, Dulaine. You were the lantern in my darkest tunnels. When the world felt heavy, you showed up with the kind of relentless optimism that defies logic. You never let me spiral alone. Our late-night calls, our spontaneous meet-ups where you listened without judgment and reminded me I was never truly stuck, kept me tethered to hope. This book exists in part because you refused to let me quit.

To my circle of old school friends, thank you for carving out time in your busy lives to drag me back into the light. Whether it was a road trip to the beach, a breakfast, or just a meal to bring us together, you reminded me what joy feels like. A special shout out goes to Sedick and Jasoda. You didn't try to "fix" me; you just showed up, again and again, with your whole hearts. Our bond, forged in classrooms decades ago, remains my shelter.

And to Rhonda: In the quiet hours when the world felt too loud, your steadiness and your unconditional love was my compass. The soothing hum of your presence keeps handing me the courage to keep going. The garden we tended in the dark is blooming. This book, like so much else, is yours. I loved you then, and I love you always.

Finally, to the readers: May these words meet you where you are, and may they remind you that light persists, even when you cannot see it.

— Robin Jackson

Notes and Sources

Introduction

Primary Source

Asimov, I. (1980, January 21). A cult of ignorance. Newsweek, 21, 19.

Historical Context

Heilbron, J. L. (2010). Galileo. Oxford University Press.
Larson, E. J. (1997). *Summer for the gods: The Scopes trial and America's continuing debate over science and religion*. Harvard University Press.

Hofstadter, R. (1963). Anti-intellectualism in American life. Knopf.

Critical Thinking & Education

Paul, R., & Elder, L. (2020). The miniature guide to critical thinking: Concepts and tools (9th ed.). Foundation for Critical Thinking.
Facione, P. A. (2020). Critical thinking: What it is and why it counts. Insight Assessment.
https://www.insightassessment.com/wp-content/uploads/ia/pdf/what-why.pdf

Media & Misinformation

Vosoughi, S., Roy, D., & Aral, S. (2018). The spread of true and false news online. Science, 359(6380), 1146–1151.
https://doi.org/10.1126/science.aap9559

Benkler, Y., Faris, R., & Roberts, H. (2018). Network propaganda: Manipulation, disinformation, and radicalization in American politics. Oxford University Press.

Cult Psychology & Group Dynamics

Lifton, R. J. (1989). Thought reform and the psychology of totalism: A study of "brainwashing" in China. University of North Carolina Press.
Singer, M. T., & Lalich, J. (1996). Cults in our midst: The hidden menace in our everyday lives. Jossey-Bass.

Anti-Intellectualism & Society

Nichols, T. (2017).The death of expertise: The campaign against established knowledge and why it matters. Oxford University Press.
McIntyre, L. (2018). Post-truth.. MIT Press.

Social Media & Echo Chambers

Pariser, E. (2011). The filter bubble: How the new personalized web is changing what we read and how we think. Penguin Books.
Sunstein, C. R. (2017). Republic: Divided democracy in the age of social media. Princeton University Press.

Additional Key Sources

Dunning, D. (2011). The Dunning-Kruger effect: On being ignorant of one's own ignorance. Advances in Experimental Social Psychology, *44*, 247–296. https://doi.org/10.1016/B978-0-12-385522-0.00005-6

Tavris, C., & Aronson, E. (2020). Mistakes were made (but not by me): Why we justify foolish beliefs, bad decisions, and hurtful acts (3rd ed.). Houghton Mifflin Harcourt.

Chapter 1

Plato. (c. 399 BCE). Apology. [Primary source on Socrates' trial and sentencing for "corrupting youth"]

Drake, S. (1978). Galileo at Work: His Scientific Biography. University of Chicago Press. [Detailed account of Galileo's conflict with the Catholic Church]

Voltaire. (1759). Candide. [Primary source mentioned in essay for satirizing blind faith]

Rousseau, J.J. (1762). Emile, or On Education. [Primary source mentioned in essay about educational approach]

Gay, P. (1995). The Enlightenment: An Interpretation. W.W. Norton & Company. [Comprehensive coverage of Enlightenment thinkers and their challenges to authority]

6. Gingerich, O. (2011). The Book Nobody Read: Chasing the Revolutions of Nicolaus Copernicus. Walker Books. [Analysis of the reception of heliocentrism]

Numbers, R.L. (2006). The Creationists: From Scientific Creationism to Intelligent Design. Harvard University Press. [Historical perspective on religion vs. science conflicts]

Reston, J. (1994). Galileo: A Life. HarperCollins. [Biography focusing on Galileo's conflict with the Church]

Nichols, T. (2017). The Death of Expertise: The Campaign Against Established Knowledge and Why It Matters. Oxford University Press. [Analysis of modern anti-intellectualism]

Rauch, J. (2021). The Constitution of Knowledge: A Defense of Truth*. Brookings Institution Press. [Examines misinformation and knowledge systems]

Hendricks, V.F., & Vestergaard, M. (2019). Reality Lost: Markets of Attention, Misinformation and Manipulation. Springer. [Analysis of misinformation in digital age]

boyd, d. (2018). "You Think You Want Media Literacy… Do You?" Data & Society. [Critical analysis of media literacy needs]

Meta. (2023). "More Speech, Fewer Mistakes" [Video announcement by Mark Zuckerberg referenced in essay]

Woolley, S. (2020). The Reality Game: How the Next Wave of Technology Will Break the Truth*. PublicAffairs. [Work by the propaganda researcher mentioned in essay]

Vosoughi, S., Roy, D., & Aral, S. (2018). "The spread of true and false news online." *Science*, 359(6380), 1146-1151. [Research on misinformation spread]

Marwick, A., & Lewis, R. (2017). "Media Manipulation and Disinformation Online." Data & Society. [Analysis of online misinformation tactics]

Hofstadter, R. (1963). Anti-intellectualism in American Life. Knopf. [Foundational study on American anti-intellectualism]

Jacoby, S. (2008). The Age of American Unreason. Pantheon Books. [Analysis of contemporary anti-intellectual trends]

Postman, N. (1985). Amusing Ourselves to Death: Public Discourse in the Age of Show Business. Penguin. [Analysis of entertainment's impact on intellectual discourse]

Furedi, F. (2004). Where Have All the Intellectuals Gone?: Confronting 21st Century Philistinism*. Continuum. [Examination of intellectualism's decline]

Facione, P.A. (1990). Critical thinking: A statement of expert consensus for purposes of educational assessment and instruction. California Academic Press. [Definitive work on critical thinking education]

McPeck, J.E. (2016). Critical Thinking and Education. Routledge. [Framework for critical thinking in educational settings]

Kahan, D.M. (2013). "Ideology, motivated reasoning, and cognitive reflection." Judgment and Decision Making, 8(4), 407-424. [Research on motivated reasoning]

Contemporary Impacts

Lewandowsky, S., Ecker, U.K.H., & Cook, J. (2017). "Beyond Misinformation: Understanding and Coping with the 'Post-Truth' Era." Journal of Applied Research in Memory and Cognition, 6(4), 353-369. [Analysis of post-truth environment]

Pariser, E. (2011). The Filter Bubble: What the Internet Is Hiding from You. Penguin Press. [Analysis of algorithmic influence on information access]

Tufekci, Z. (2017). Twitter and Tear Gas: The Power and Fragility of Networked Protest. Yale University Press. [Analysis of social media's influence on discourse]

Chapter 2

Asimov, I. (1980). "A Cult of Ignorance." Newsweek, January 21, 1980. [Referenced directly in the essay introduction]

Paine, T. (1776). Common Sense. [Historical reference

mentioned in the "Everyman" section]

Somin, I. (2016). Democracy and Political Ignorance: Why Smaller Government Is Smarter. Stanford University Press. [Analysis of political ignorance in democratic systems]

Kahneman, D. (2011). Thinking, Fast and Slow. Farrar, Straus and Giroux. [Exploration of cognitive biases and intuitive vs. rational thinking]

Populism and Anti-Intellectualism in Politics

Mudde, C., & Kaltwasser, C. R. (2017). Populism: A Very Short Introduction*. Oxford University Press. [Framework for understanding populist movements]

Oliver, J. E., & Rahn, W. M. (2016). "Rise of the Trumpenvolk: Populism in the 2016 Election." The ANNALS of the American Academy of Political and Social Science, 667(1), 189–206. [Analysis of Trump's populist appeal]

Hunter, W., & Power, T. J. (2019). "Bolsonaro and Brazil's Illiberal Backlash." Journal of Democracy, 30(1), 68-82. [Analysis of Bolsonaro's leadership style and rhetoric]

Richwine, J. (2009). The Burden of 'Acting White': Anti-Intellectualism and Black Identity*. Heritage Foundation. [Examination of cultural anti-intellectualism and its impacts]

Media and Misinformation

Limbaugh, R. (2013). Rush Revere and the Brave Pilgrims: Time-Travel Adventures with Exceptional Americans. Threshold Editions. [Primary source for analyzing conservative media rhetoric]

Carlson, T. (2018). Ship of Fools: How a Selfish Ruling Class

Is Bringing America to the Brink of Revolution. Free Press. [Primary source from media figure mentioned in essay]

Boykoff, M. T., & Boykoff, J. M. (2004). "Balance as bias: Global warming and the US prestige press." Global Environmental Change, 14(2), 125-136. [Analysis of false equivalency in media coverage]

Kata, A. (2012). "Anti-vaccine activists, Web 2.0, and the postmodern paradigm—An overview of tactics and tropes used online by the anti-vaccination movement." Vaccine, 30(25), 3778-3789. [Examination of anti-vaccine rhetoric]

Seth, S., Glendinning, S., & Forgan, S. (2021). "Jenny McCarthy's Activism, Celebrities, and Autism's Uncertain Causes." In Global Perspectives on Health Communication in the Age of Social Media (pp. 236-256). [Analysis of celebrity influence on vaccine hesitancy]

Brexit and Political Strategy

Clarke, H. D., Goodwin, M., & Whiteley, P. (2017). Brexit: Why Britain Voted to Leave the European Union. Cambridge University Press. [Analysis of Brexit campaign strategies]

Shipman, T. (2016). All Out War: The Full Story of How Brexit Sank Britain's Political Class. William Collins. [Detailed account of the Brexit campaign, including "Project Fear" rhetoric]

Reboot Foundation. (2018). The State of Critical Thinking. [Study cited in essay about critical thinking skills]

Digital Misinformation

Center for Countering Digital Hate. (2021). The Disinformation Dozen: Why platforms must act on twelve leading online anti-vaxxers. [Study cited in essay about 12 anti-vaccine accounts]

Pariser, E. (2011). The Filter Bubble: What the Internet Is Hiding from You. Penguin Press. [Analysis of algorithmic influence on information consumption]

Vosoughi, S., Roy, D., & Aral, S. (2018). "The spread of true and false news online." Science, 359(6380), 1146-1151. [Research on misinformation spread patterns]

Benkler, Y., Faris, R., & Roberts, H. (2018). Network Propaganda: Manipulation, Disinformation, and Radicalization in American Politics. Oxford University Press. [Comprehensive analysis of media ecosystems and misinformation]

Anti-Vaccine Movement and Health Consequences

Texas Department of State Health Services. (2025). Measles Outbreak Report: Texas and New Mexico. [Source for the 2025 measles outbreak mentioned in essay]

World Health Organization. (2019). Measles Outbreak in Samoa: Situation Report. [Source for Samoa measles statistics]

Hussain, A., Ali, S., Ahmed, M., & Hussain, S. (2018). "The Anti-vaccination Movement: A Regression in Modern Medicine." Cureus, 10(7), e2919. [Analysis of anti-vaccination movement]

Nyhan, B., Reifler, J., Richey, S., & Freed, G. L. (2014). "Effective Messages in Vaccine Promotion: A Randomized Trial." Pediatrics, 133(4), e835-e842. [Research on vaccine messaging effectiveness]

Climate Change Denial

Oreskes, N., & Conway, E. M. (2010). Merchants of Doubt: How a Handful of Scientists Obscured the Truth on Issues from Tobacco Smoke to Global Warming. Bloomsbury Press. [Definitive work on organized climate denial]

Dunlap, R. E., & McCright, A. M. (2011). "Organized Climate Change Denial." In J. S. Dryzek, R. B. Norgaard, & D. Schlosberg (Eds.), The Oxford Handbook of Climate Change and Society (pp. 144-160). Oxford University Press. [Analysis of climate denial organizations]

Brulle, R. J. (2014). "Institutionalizing delay: foundation funding and the creation of U.S. climate change counter-movement organizations." Climatic Change, 122(4), 681-694. [Research on funding of climate denial organizations like Heartland Institute]

COVID-19 Politicization

Bull-Otterson, L., et al. (2020). "Hydroxychloroquine and Chloroquine Prescribing Patterns by Provider Specialty Following Initial Reports of Potential Benefit for COVID-19 Treatment." MMWR Morbidity and Mortality Weekly Report, 69, 478–481. [Data on hydroxychloroquine usage after Trump endorsement]

Evanega, S., Lynas, M., Adams, J., & Smolenyak, K. (2020). Coronavirus misinformation: quantifying sources and themes in the COVID-19 'infodemic'. Cornell Alliance for Science. [Analysis of COVID-19 misinformation sources]

Motta, M., Stecula, D., & Farhart, C. (2020). "How Right-Leaning Media Coverage of COVID-19 Facilitated the Spread of Misinformation in the Early Stages of the

Pandemic in the U.S." Canadian Journal of Political Science*, 53(2), 335-342. [Analysis of partisan media coverage of COVID-19]

Solutions and Recommendations

Facione, P. A. (2020). Critical Thinking: What It Is and Why It Counts. Insight Assessment. [Framework for critical thinking education]

Wineburg, S., & McGrew, S. (2019). Lateral Reading: Reading Less and Learning More When Evaluating Digital Information. Stanford History Education Group. [Digital literacy techniques]

Lewandowsky, S., Ecker, U. K. H., Seifert, C. M., Schwarz, N., & Cook, J. (2012). "Misinformation and Its Correction: Continued Influence and Successful Debiasing." Psychological Science in the Public Interest, 13(3), 106-131. [Research on correcting misinformation]

boyd, d. (2018). "You Think You Want Media Literacy... Do You?" Data & Society. [Critical analysis of media literacy approaches]

Levitin, D. J. (2016). A Field Guide to Lies: Critical Thinking in the Information Age. Dutton. [Practical guide to critical thinking and information evaluation]

Chapter 3

Philosophical Foundations

Mill, J.S. (1859). On Liberty. [Primary source extensively quoted in the essay]

Mill, J.S. (1869). The Subjection of Women. [Additional work by Mill that expands on his views of liberty and equality]

Berlin, I. (2002). Liberty: Incorporating Four Essays on Liberty. Oxford University Press. [Analysis of Mill's concepts of liberty]

Cohen-Almagor, R. (2017). "J.S. Mill's Boundaries of Freedom of Expression: A Critique." Philosophy, 92(4), 565-596. [Critical examination of Mill's free speech principles]

Habermas, J. (1989). The Structural Transformation of the Public Sphere: An Inquiry into a Category of Bourgeois Society. MIT Press. [Theoretical framework for understanding public discourse]

The "Marketplace of Ideas" Concept

Abrams v. United States, 250 U.S. 616 (1919). [Justice Holmes' dissent introducing the "marketplace of ideas" concept]

Gordon, J. (1997). "John Stuart Mill and the 'Marketplace of Ideas'." Social Theory and Practice, 23(2), 235-249. [Historical analysis of the concept]

Napoli, P.M. (1999). "The Marketplace of Ideas Metaphor in Communications Regulation." Journal of Communication, 49(4), 151-169. [Analysis of the concept's application in modern media]

Goldman, A.I., & Cox, J.C. (1996). "Speech, Truth, and the Free Market for Ideas." Legal Theory, 2(1), 1-32. [Exploration of economic metaphors for truth-seeking discourse]

Cognitive Biases and the Dunning-Kruger Effect

Kruger, J., & Dunning, D. (1999). "Unskilled and unaware of

it: How difficulties in recognizing one's own incompetence lead to inflated self-assessments." Journal of Personality and Social Psychology, 77(6), 1121-1134. [Original research on the Dunning-Kruger effect]

Dunning, D. (2011). "The Dunning-Kruger Effect: On Being Ignorant of One's Own Ignorance." Advances in Experimental Social Psychology, 44, 247-296. [Expanded analysis by one of the original researchers]

West, R.F., Meserve, R.J., & Stanovich, K.E. (2012). "Cognitive sophistication does not attenuate the bias blind spot." Journal of Personality and Social Psychology, 103(3), 506-519. [Research on metacognitive limitations]

Anson, I.G. (2018). "Partisanship, Political Knowledge, and the Dunning-Kruger Effect." Political Psychology, 39(5), 1173-1192. [Application of Dunning-Kruger to political knowledge]

Social Media and Misinformation

Vosoughi, S., Roy, D., & Aral, S. (2018). "The spread of true and false news online." Science, 359(6380), 1146-1151. [MIT study cited in the essay about false news spreading faster]

Bail, C.A., et al. (2018). "Exposure to opposing views on social media can increase political polarization." Proceedings of the National Academy of Sciences, 115(37), 9216-9221. [Research on echo chambers]

Broniatowski, D.A., et al. (2018). "Weaponized Health Communication: Twitter Bots and Russian Trolls Amplify the Vaccine Debate." American Journal of Public Health, 108(10), 1378-1384. [Study on social media manipulation]

Del Vicario, M., et al. (2016). "The spreading of misinformation online." Proceedings of the National

Academy of Sciences, 113(3), 554-559. [Analysis of information cascades on social media]

Noble, S.U. (2018). Algorithms of Oppression: How Search Engines Reinforce Racism. NYU Press. [Critical analysis of algorithmic influence]

Climate Change Debate and False Equivalence

 Boykoff, M.T., & Boykoff, J.M. (2004). "Balance as bias: global warming and the US prestige press." Global Environmental Change, 14(2), 125-136. [Analysis of false balance in climate change reporting]

Cook, J., et al. (2016). "Consensus on consensus: a synthesis of consensus estimates on human-caused global warming." Environmental Research Letters, 11(4), 048002. [Meta-analysis of scientific consensus]

Oreskes, N. (2004). "The Scientific Consensus on Climate Change." Science, 306(5702), 1686. [Foundational study on scientific consensus]

Lewandowsky, S., Oreskes, N., Risbey, J.S., Newell, B.R., & Smithson, M. (2015). "Seepage: Climate change denial and its effect on the scientific community." Global Environmental Change, 33, 1-13. [Analysis of how denialism affects scientific discourse]

COVID-19 and Public Health

Gyenes, N., & Mina, A.X. (2018). "How Misinfodemics Spread Disease." The Atlantic. [Analysis of health misinformation]

Burki, T. (2020). "The online anti-vaccine movement in the age of COVID-19." The Lancet Digital Health, 2(10), e504-e505. [Study on anti-vaccine movements during the pandemic]

Motta, M., Callaghan, T., & Sylvester, S. (2018). "Knowing less but presuming more: Dunning-Kruger effects and the endorsement of anti-vaccine policy attitudes." Social Science & Medicine, 211, 274-281. [Linking Dunning-Kruger to anti-vaccine attitudes]

Cinelli, M., et al. (2020). "The COVID-19 social media infodemic." Scientific Reports, 10, 16598. [Analysis of COVID-19 misinformation on social media]

Erosion of Expertise and "Opinionism"

Nichols, T. (2017). The Death of Expertise: The Campaign Against Established Knowledge and Why it Matters. Oxford University Press. [Comprehensive analysis of anti-intellectualism]

Hoffman, S.J., & Tan, C. (2015). "Biological, psychological and social processes that explain celebrities' influence on patients' health-related behaviors." Archives of Public Health, 73(1), 3. [Study on celebrity influence]

Kakutani, M. (2018). The Death of Truth: Notes on Falsehood in the Age of Trump. Tim Duggan Books. [Analysis of "post-truth" culture]

Collins, H., & Evans, R. (2007). Rethinking Expertise. University of Chicago Press. [Sociological analysis of expertise]

Media Literacy and Critical Thinking

Silverblatt, A., Miller, D.C., Smith, J., & Brown, N. (2014). Media Literacy: Keys to Interpreting Media Messages. Praeger. [Framework for media literacy education]

Hobbs, R. (2010). "Digital and Media Literacy: A Plan of Action." The Aspen Institute Communications and Society Program. [Strategic approach to media literacy]

Facione, P.A. (1990). Critical thinking: A statement of expert consensus for purposes of educational assessment and instruction. California Academic Press. [Foundational framework for critical thinking]

Miller, J.W. (2005). "Teaching Critical Thinking in the Social Studies Classroom: A Model for Global Education for the 21st Century." The Social Studies, 96(6), 257-261. [Practical approach to teaching critical thinking]

Intellectual Humility

Leary, M.R., et al. (2017). "Cognitive and Interpersonal Features of Intellectual Humility." Personality and Social Psychology Bulletin, 43(6), 793-813. [Research on intellectual humility]

Church, I.M., & Samuelson, P.L. (2017). Intellectual Humility: An Introduction to the Philosophy and Science. Bloomsbury Academic. [Comprehensive overview of intellectual humility]

Deffler, S.A., Leary, M.R., & Hoyle, R.H. (2016). "Knowing what you know: Intellectual humility and judgments of recognition memory." Personality and Individual Differences, 96, 255-259. [Empirical study of intellectual humility]

Krumrei-Mancuso, E.J., & Rouse, S.V. (2016). "The Development and Validation of the Comprehensive Intellectual Humility Scale." Journal of Personality Assessment, 98(2), 209-221. [Measurement of intellectual humility]

Chapter 4

General Media and Misinformation

Asimov, Isaac. "A Cult of Ignorance." Newsweek, January 21, 1980.

Vosoughi, Soroush, Deb Roy, and Sinan Aral. "The Spread of True and False News Online." Science 359, no. 6380 (2018): 1146-1151. [MIT study showing false news spreads six times faster than true stories on Twitter]

The Lancet Digital Health. "The Online Anti-vaccine Movement in the Age of COVID-19." The Lancet Digital Health 2, no. 10 (2020): e504-e505.

Gallup. "Americans' Trust in Media Remains Near Record Low." September 2021.

Israel-Palestinian Conflict

Said, Edward W. Covering Islam: How the Media and the Experts Determine How We See the Rest of the World. Vintage Books, 1997.

Philo, Greg, and Mike Berry. Bad News from Israel. Pluto Press, 2004.

Zelizer, Barbie, et al. Journalism After September 11. Routledge, 2011.

White Genocide Myth in South Africa

Africa Check. "Are White Farmers Being Killed 'Like Flies' in South Africa?" June 2018.

Africa Check. "The Statistical Reality of Crime in South

Africa." Annual Crime Statistics Report, 2023.

Lancaster, Lizette. "Unpacking the Statistics on Farm Attacks and Murders." Institute for Security Studies, South Africa, 2024.

Chutel, Lynsey. "Farm Murders in South Africa: Unpacking the Media Narrative." Foreign Policy, 2018.

Newham, Gareth. "Crime and Race in Post-Apartheid South Africa." Institute for Security Studies, 2024.

Walsh, Joe. "White Genocide: A Dangerous Myth." The Guardian, 2024.

South African Government. "Land Reform Statistics and Policy." Department of Agriculture, Land Reform and Rural Development, 2025.

Iraq War and WMDs

Miller, Greg. "The Intelligence Community and the Iraq War." Washington Post, 2016.

Gordon, Michael R., and Judith Miller. "Threats and Responses: The Iraqis; U.S. Says Hussein Intensifies Quest for A-Bomb Parts." The New York Times, September 8, 2002.

Kull, Steven, Clay Ramsay, and Evan Lewis. "Misperceptions, the Media, and the Iraq War." Political Science Quarterly 118, no. 4 (2003): 569-598.

Russian Interference in 2016 U.S. Election

United States Senate Select Committee on Intelligence. "Russian Active Measures Campaigns and Interference in the 2016 U.S. Election." 2019.

Mueller, Robert S. "Report on the Investigation into Russian Interference in the 2016 Presidential Election." U.S. Department of Justice, 2019.

Howard, Philip N., et al. "The IRA, Social Media and Political Polarization in the United States, 2012-2018." Computational Propaganda Research Project, Oxford University, 2018.

Corporate Media Manipulation

Oreskes, Naomi, and Erik M. Conway. Merchants of Doubt: How a Handful of Scientists Obscured the Truth on Issues from Tobacco Smoke to Global Warming. Bloomsbury Publishing, 2011.

Michaels, David. Doubt is Their Product: How Industry's Assault on Science Threatens Your Health. Oxford University Press, 2008.

Media Literacy and Solutions

Hobbs, Renee. Mind Over Media: Propaganda Education for a Digital Age. W. W. Norton & Company, 2020.

Silverman, Craig. Verification Handbook: A Definitive Guide to Verifying Digital Content for Emergency Coverage. European Journalism Centre, 2014.

Newton, Julianne H. The Burden of Visual Truth: The Role of Photojournalism in Mediating Reality. Lawrence Erlbaum Associates, 2001.

Chapter 5

Military-Entertainment Complex

Robb, David. Operation Hollywood: How the Pentagon Shapes and Censors the Movies. Prometheus Books, 2004.

Der Derian, James. Virtuous War: Mapping the Military-Industrial-Media-Entertainment Network. Routledge, 2009.

Jenkins, Tricia. The CIA in Hollywood: How the Agency Shapes Film and Television. University of Texas Press, 2016.

Alford, Matthew. Reel Power: Hollywood Cinema and American Supremacy. Pluto Press, 2010.

Boggs, Carl, and Tom Pollard. The Hollywood War Machine: U.S. Militarism and Popular Culture. Routledge, 2016.

Stahl, Roger. Militainment, Inc.: War, Media, and Popular Culture*. Routledge, 2009.

United States Department of Defense. "Film Liaison Office Guidelines and Procedures." Pentagon, 2020.

Suid, Lawrence H. Guts and Glory: The Making of the American Military Image in Film. University Press of Kentucky, 2002.

Arab and Muslim Stereotypes in Film

Shaheen, Jack G. Reel Bad Arabs: How Hollywood Vilifies a People. Olive Branch Press, 2009.

Said, Edward W. Covering Islam: How the Media and the Experts Determine How We See the Rest of the World. Vintage Books, 1997.

Alsultany, Evelyn. Arabs and Muslims in the Media: Race and Representation After 9/11. NYU Press, 2012.

Semmerling, Tim Jon. "Evil" Arabs in American Popular Film: Orientalist Fear. University of Texas Press, 2006.

Kumar, Deepa. Islamophobia and the Politics of Empire. Haymarket Books, 2021.

Khatib, Lina. Filming the Modern Middle East: Politics in the Cinemas of Hollywood and the Arab World. I.B. Tauris, 2006.

Rana, Junaid. Terrifying Muslims: Race and Labor in the South Asian Diaspora. Duke University Press, 2011.

Hollywood and Soft Propaganda

Kellner, Douglas. Cinema Wars: Hollywood Film and Politics in the Bush-Cheney Era. Wiley-Blackwell, 2010.

Davis, Elmer. War Information and American Propaganda. Princeton University Press, 1943.

Herman, Edward S., and Noam Chomsky. Manufacturing Consent: The Political Economy of the Mass Media. Pantheon Books, 2002.

Shaw, Tony, and Denise J. Youngblood. Cinematic Cold War: The American and Soviet Struggle for Hearts and Minds. University Press of Kansas, 2010.

Giroux, Henry A. Breaking in to the Movies: Film and the Culture of Politics. Blackwell Publishers, 2002.

Zajonc, Robert B. "Attitudinal Effects of Mere Exposure." Journal of Personality and Social Psychology 9, no. 2 (1968): 1-27. [Mere exposure effect study]

Pötzsch, Holger. "The Emergence of iWar: Changing Practices and Perceptions of Military Engagement in a

Digital Era." New Media & Society 17, no. 1 (2015): 78-95.

Diversity and Representation in Film

Smith, Stacy L., et al. "Inequality in 1,200 Popular Films: Examining Portrayals of Gender, Race/Ethnicity, LGBTQ & Disability from 2007 to 2018." USC Annenberg Inclusion Initiative, 2019.

Benshoff, Harry M., and Sean Griffin. America on Film: Representing Race, Class, Gender, and Sexuality at the Movies. Wiley-Blackwell, 2021.

hooks, bell. Reel to Real: Race, Class and Sex at the Movies. Routledge, 2008.

Gray, Herman. Cultural Moves: African Americans and the Politics of Representation*. University of California Press, 2005.

Dyer, Richard. White: Essays on Race and Culture. Routledge, 1997.

Gabriel, Teshome H. Third Cinema in the Third World: The Aesthetics of Liberation. UMI Research Press, 1982.

Films and Shows Referenced

Scott, Ridley, director. Black Hawk Down. Columbia Pictures, 2001.

Bay, Michael, director. Transformers. Paramount Pictures, 2007.

Bigelow, Kathryn, director. Zero Dark Thirty. Columbia Pictures, 2012.

Stone, Oliver, director. Platoon. Orion Pictures, 1986.

Kosinski, Joseph, director. Top Gun: Maverick. Paramount Pictures, 2022.

Cameron, James, director. True Lies. 20th Century Fox, 1994.

Musker, John, and Ron Clements, directors. Aladdin. Walt Disney Pictures, 1992.

Berg, Peter, director. The Kingdom. Universal Pictures, 2007.

Eastwood, Clint, director. American Sniper. Warner Bros. Pictures, 2014.

King, Michael Patrick, director. Sex and the City 2. Warner Bros. Pictures, 2010.

Youssef, Ramy, creator. Ramy. Hulu, 2019-present.

Ali, Adil El Arbi, Bilall Fallah, et al., directors. Ms. Marvel. Disney+, 2022.

Zaillian, Steven, and Richard Price, creators. The Night Of. HBO, 2016.

Gordon, Howard, and Alex Gansa, creators. Homeland. Showtime, 2011-2020.

Curtiz, Michael, director. Casablanca. Warner Bros. Pictures, 1942.

Wyler, William, director. Mrs. Miniver. Metro-Goldwyn-Mayer, 1942.

Peele, Jordan, director. Get Out. Universal Pictures, 2017.

Bong Joon-ho, director. Parasite. CJ Entertainment, 2019.

Kwan, Daniel, and Daniel Scheinert, directors. Everything Everywhere All at Once. A24, 2022.

Brunson, Quinta, creator. Abbott Elementary. ABC, 2021-present.

Chapter 6

Nichols, Tom. The Death of Expertise: The Campaign Against Established Knowledge and Why it Matters. Oxford University Press, 2017.

Dunning, David. Self-Insight: Roadblocks and Detours on the Path to Knowing Thyself. Psychology Press, 2005.

Sunstein, Cass R. On Rumors: How Falsehoods Spread, Why We Believe Them, and What Can Be Done. Princeton University Press, 2009.

Kahneman, Daniel. Thinking, Fast and Slow. Farrar, Straus and Giroux, 2011.

Academic Papers & Reports:

Kruger, Justin, and David Dunning. "Unskilled and Unaware of It: How Difficulties in Recognizing One's Own Incompetence Lead to Inflated Self-Assessments." Journal of Personality and Social Psychology, vol. 77, no. 6, 1999, pp. 1121–1134.

Lewandowsky, Stephan, et al. "Misinformation and Its Correction: Continued Influence and Successful Debiasing." Psychological Science in the Public Interest, vol. 13, no. 3, 2012, pp. 106–131.

Bessi, Alessandro, and Emilio Ferrara. "Social Bots Distort

the 2016 U.S. Presidential Election Online Discussion." First Monday, vol. 21, no. 11, 2016.

Case Studies & Industry Reports:

Financial Crisis Inquiry Commission. The Financial Crisis Inquiry Report. U.S. Government Printing Office, 2011.

Carreyrou, John. Bad Blood: Secrets and Lies in a Silicon Valley Startup. Knopf, 2018.

Final Committee Report on Boeing 737 MAX Failures. U.S. House of Representatives Committee on Transportation and Infrastructure, 2020.

Articles & Media Sources:

Nyhan, Brendan, and Jason Reifler. "When Corrections Fail: The Persistence of Political Misperceptions." *Political Behavior*, vol. 32, no. 2, 2010, pp. 303–330.

Zuckerman, Ethan. "The Cute Cat Theory of Digital Activism." Journal of Information Technology & Politics*, vol. 8, no. 2, 2011, pp. 161–180.

Motta, Matthew. "The Dynamics and Political Implications of Anti-Intellectualism in the United States." American Politics Research, vol. 46, no. 3, 2018, pp. 465–498.

Pennycook, Gordon, and David G. Rand. "The Implied Truth Effect: Attaching Warnings to a Subset of Fake News Stories Increases Perceived Accuracy of Stories Without Warnings." Management Science, vol. 66, no. 11, 2020, pp. 4944–4957.

Chapter 7

Psychology of Conspiracy Thinking

Douglas, K. M., & Sutton, R. M. (2018). Why Conspiracy Theories Matter: A Social Psychological Analysis. Social and **Personality Psychology Compass.**

van Prooijen, J.-W. (2020). An Existential Threat Model of Conspiracy Theories. European Psychologist.

Hogg, M. A. (2014). From Uncertainty to Extremism: Social Categorization and Identity Processes.* Current Directions in Psychological Science.

Jolley, D., & Douglas, K. M. (2014). The Effects of Anti-Vaccine Conspiracy Theories on Vaccination Intentions. PLOS ONE.

Historical Context of Conspiracy Theories

Hofstadter, R. (1964). The Paranoid Style in American Politics. Harper's Magazine.

Barkun, M. (2013). A Culture of Conspiracy: Apocalyptic Visions in Contemporary America. University of California Press.

Pipes, D. (1997). Conspiracy: How the Paranoid Style Flourishes and Where It Comes From. Free Press.

David Icke & Reptilian Elite Narratives

Robertson, D. G. (2016). Conspiracy Theories and the Study of Alternative Spiritualities. Journal of Contemporary Religion.

QAnon

Rothschild, M. (2021). The Storm Is Upon Us: How QAnon Became a Movement, Cult, and Conspiracy Theory of Everything. Melville House.

Anti-Defamation League (ADL). (2021). QAnon: A Glossary of Terms and References.

Anti-Vaccine Movement

Offit, P. A. (2011). Deadly Choices: How the Anti-Vaccine Movement Threatens Us All. Basic Books.

Larson, H. J. (2020). Stuck: How Vaccine Rumors Start—and Why They Don't Go Away. Oxford University Press.

Climate Change Denial

Oreskes, N., & Conway, E. M. (2010). Merchants of Doubt: How a Handful of Scientists Obscured the Truth on Issues from Tobacco Smoke to Climate Change. Bloomsbury Press.

Dunlap, R. E., & McCright, A. M. (2015). Challenging Climate Change: The Denial Countermovement. In Climate Change and Society. Oxford University Press.

Technology & Social Media Amplification

Tufekci, Z. (2018). YouTube, the Great Radicalizer. The New York Times.

Data & Society. (2018). Media Manipulation and Disinformation Online

Vosoughi, S., et al. (2018). The Spread of True and False News Online. Science.

Combating Conspiracy Theories

UNESCO. (2021). Media and Information Literacy Curriculum for Educators and Learners.

Stanford History Education Group. (2019). Civic Online Reasoning Curriculum.

Lewandowsky, S., et al. (2017). Beyond Misinformation: Understanding and Coping with the "Post-Truth" Era.* Journal of Applied Research in Memory and Cognition.

Nyhan, B., et al. (2020). Effective Messages in Vaccine Promotion: A Randomized Trial. Pediatrics.

Storytelling & Narrative Strategies

Heath, C., & Heath, D. (2007). Made to Stick: Why Some Ideas Survive and Others Die. Random House.

van der Linden, S. (2022). Foolproof: Why Misinformation Infects Our Minds and How to Build Immunity. WW Norton.

Key Repositories for Further Research

JSTOR, PubMed, and Google Scholar for peer-reviewed studies.

SAGE Journals' Social Psychological and Personality Science for empirical psychology research.

Chapter 8

Education as Enlightenment & Critical Thinking

Dewey, J. (1916). Democracy and Education. Macmillan.

Nussbaum, M. C. (2010). Not for Profit: Why Democracy Needs the Humanities. Princeton University Press.

Freire, P. (1970). Pedagogy of the Oppressed. Continuum.

Darling-Hammond, L. (2010). The Flat World and Education: How America's Commitment to Equity Will Determine Our Future. Teachers College Press.

Education as Oppression: Historical & Contemporary Case Studies

Apartheid Education

Kallaway, P. (Ed.). (2002). The History of Education Under Apartheid, 1948–1994. Peter Lang.

Mandela, N. (1994). Long Walk to Freedom. Little, Brown.

Residential Schools & Colonial Education

Truth and Reconciliation Commission of Canada. (2015).Honouring the Truth, Reconciling for the Future.

Adams, D. W. (1995). Education for Extinction: American Indians and the Boarding School Experience. University Press of Kansas.

Battiste, M. (2013). Decolonizing Education: Nourishing the Learning Spirit. Purich Publishing.

Global Colonial Education

Fanon, F. (1961). The Wretched of the Earth. Grove Press.

Memmi, A. (1965). The Colonizer and the Colonized. Beacon Press.

Curriculum Control & Censorship

Apple, M. W. (2004). Ideology and Curriculum. Routledge.

Loewen, J. W. (1995). Lies My Teacher Told Me: Everything Your American History Textbook Got Wrong. The New Press.

American Educational Research Association. (2021). Statement on Legislative Efforts to Restrict Education About Racism.

Systemic Inequities: Funding, Testing, & Access

Kozol, J. (1991). Savage Inequalities: Children in America's Schools. Crown.

Ravitch, D. (2010). The Death and Life of the Great American School System. Basic Books.

OECD. (2018). Equity in Education: Breaking Down Barriers to Social Mobility.

Technology & Surveillance in Education

Selwyn, N. (2022). Education and Technology: Key Issues and Debates. Bloomsbury.

UNESCO. (2021). AI and Education: Guidance for Policy-Makers.

Lifelong Learning & Resistance

Illich, I. (1971). Deschooling Society. Harper & Row.

Brookfield, S. D. (2005). The Power of Critical Theory for Adult Learning and Teaching. Open University Press.

OECD. (2019). Getting Skills Right: Future-Ready Adult Learning Systems.

Key Repositories for Further Research

ERIC (Education Resources Information Center) for peer-reviewed education studies.

Project MUSE for humanities-focused analyses of education policy.

JSTOR for historical and contemporary educational research.

Chapter 9

Burns, D. D. (1980). Feeling Good: The New Mood Therapy. HarperCollins.

Gerlich, M., et al. (2023). AI Use and Declining Critical Thinking Skills: A Correlational Study. SBS Swiss Business School Journal of Cognitive Studies, 15(4), 231-247.

Haidt, J. (2012). The Righteous Mind: Why Good People Are Divided by Politics and Religion. Vintage.

Kumar, R. (2022). AI in Hiring: The Perils of Automation in Professional Evaluation. Harvard Business Review, 100(2), 78-89.

Leahy, R. L., Tirch, D., & Napolitano, L. A. (2011). Emotion Regulation in Psychotherapy: A Practitioner's Guide. Guilford Press.

Pariser, E. (2011). The Filter Bubble: How the New Personalized Web Is Changing What We Read and How We Think. Penguin.

Risko, E. F., & Gilbert, S. J. (2016). Cognitive Offloading. Trends in Cognitive Sciences, 20(9), 676-688.

Sunstein, C. R. (2017). Republic: Divided Democracy in the Age of Social Media. Princeton University Press.

Vosoughi, S., Roy, D., & Aral, S. (2018). The Spread of True and False News Online. Science, 359(6380), 1146-1151.

Chapter 10

Allen, J. (2006). Rabble-Rouser for Peace: The Authorized Biography of Desmond Tutu. Free Press.

Armstrong, K. (1993). A History of God: The 4,000-Year Quest of Judaism, Christianity and Islam. Knopf.

Carson, C. (2005). The Autobiography of Martin Luther King, Jr. Grand Central Publishing.

Draper, J. W. (1874). History of the Conflict Between Religion and Science. Appleton.

Finocchiaro, M. A. (1989). The Galileo Affair: A Documentary History. University of California Press.

Harris, S. (2004). The End of Faith: Religion, Terror, and the Future of Reason. Norton.

Hoffer, E. (1951). The True Believer: Thoughts on the Nature of Mass Movements. Harper & Row.

Hotez, P. (2020). Preventing the Next Pandemic: Vaccine Diplomacy in a Time of Anti-Science. Johns Hopkins University Press.

Madison, J. (1822). Letter to Edward Livingston.

Chapter 11

Benkler, Y., Faris, R., & Roberts, H. (2018). Network Propaganda: Manipulation, Disinformation, and Radicalization in American Politics. Oxford University Press.

Carr, N. (2010). The Shallows: What the Internet Is Doing to Our Brains. W.W. Norton & Company.

Castells, M. (2001). The Internet Galaxy: Reflections on the Internet, Business, and Society. Oxford University Press.

Eisenstein, E. (1979). The Printing Press as an Agent of Change. Cambridge University Press.

Gillespie, T. (2018). Custodians of the Internet: Platforms, Content Moderation, and the Hidden Decisions That Shape Social Media. Yale University Press.

Habermas, J. (1989). The Structural Transformation of the Public Sphere. MIT Press.

Kahne, J., & Bowyer, B. (2017). Educating for Democracy in a Partisan Age: Confronting the Challenges of Motivated Reasoning and Misinformation. American Educational Research Journal, 54(1), 3-34.

Newport, C. (2019). Digital Minimalism: Choosing a Focused Life in a Noisy World. Portfolio.

Nichols, T. (2017). The Death of Expertise: The Campaign Against Established Knowledge and Why It Matters. Oxford University Press.

Pariser, E. (2011). The Filter Bubble: How the New

Personalized Web Is Changing What We Read and How We Think. Penguin Books.

Sunstein, C. R. (2001). Republic.com. Princeton University Press.

Vaidhyanathan, S. (2018). Antisocial Media: How Facebook Disconnects Us and Undermines Democracy. Oxford University Press.

Wardle, C., & Derakhshan, H. (2017). Information Disorder: Toward an Interdisciplinary Framework for Research and Policy Making. Council of Europe.

Zuboff, S. (2019). The Age of Surveillance Capitalism: The Fight for a Human Future at the New Frontier of Power. PublicAffairs.

Chapter 12

Political Exploitation of Ignorance & Propaganda

Chomsky, N. (1988). Manufacturing consent: The political economy of the mass media. Pantheon Books.
Stanley, J. (2015). How propaganda works. Princeton University Press.
Arendt, H. (1951). The origins of totalitarianism. Schocken Books.

Historical Case Studies

Ancient Rome: Bread and Circuses

Juvenal. (1998). Satire X. In P. Green (Trans.), The sixteen satires (pp. 207–219). Penguin Classics. (Original work published 2nd century CE)

Suetonius. (1957). The twelve caesars (R. Graves, Trans.). Penguin Classics. (Original work published 121 CE)

Nazi Germany & Goebbels' Propaganda

Kershaw, I. (2001). The "Hitler myth": Image and reality in the Third Reich*. Oxford University Press.

Herf, J. (2006). The Jewish enemy: Nazi propaganda during World War II and the Holocaust*. Harvard University Press.

McCarthyism & Red Scare

Schrecker, E. (1998). Many are the crimes: McCarthyism in America. Princeton University Press.

Haynes, J. E. (2000). Red scare or red menace? American communism and anticommunism in the Cold War era. Ivan R. Dee.

 Modern Case Studies

South Africa's BELA Bill (2021–2024)

South African Department of Basic Education. (2021). Basic Education Laws Amendment (BELA) Bill*. Government Gazette.

Jansen, J. (2023). Language politics and the BELA Bill controversy. South African Journal of Education, 43 (2), 123–145. https://doi.org/10.15700/saje.v43n2a2201
Human Rights Watch. (2024). Transgender rights in South African schools. https://www.hrw.org/reports/south-africa-transgender-rights-2024

Brexit & Immigration Fear-Mongering

Hobolt, S. B. (2016). The Brexit vote: A divided nation, a

divided continent. Journal of European Public Policy, 23 (9), 1259–1277.
https://doi.org/10.1080/13501763.2016.1225785

Goodwin, M., & Milazzo, C. (2017). Taking back control? Investigating the role of immigration in the 2016 Brexit vote. British Journal of Political Science, 47 (3), 451–476.
https://doi.org/10.1017/S0007123415000065

Media, Technology, & Disinformation

Benkler, Y., Faris, R., & Roberts, H. (2018). Network propaganda: Manipulation, disinformation, and radicalization in American politics. Oxford University Press.

Wardle, C., & Derakhshan, H. (2017). Information disorder: Toward an interdisciplinary framework for research and policy. Council of Europe.
https://edoc.coe.int/en/media/7495-information-disorder-report-english-version.html

Voter Suppression & Gerrymandering

Anderson, C. (2020). One person, no vote: How voter suppression is destroying our democracy*. Bloomsbury.
Wang, T. (2022). The politics of voter suppression: Defending and expanding Americans' right to vote. Cornell University Press.

Solutions & Resistance

Levitsky, S., & Ziblatt, D. (2018). How democracies die. Crown.
UNESCO. (2023). Media and information literacy curriculum for educators and learners.
https://unesdoc.unesco.org/ark:/48223/pf0000382301

Key Repositories

HeinOnline. (n.d.). Legal database.
https://home.heinonline.org
Project MUSE. (n.d.). Academic journals.
https://muse.jhu.edu
South African Government. (n.d.). Government publications.
https://www.gov.za/documents

Chapter 13

Historical & Theoretical Foundations

Hoffer, E. (1951). The true believer: Thoughts on the nature
of mass movements. Harper & Brothers.

Orwell, G. (1949). 1984. Secker & Warburg.

Festinger, L. (1957). A theory of cognitive dissonance.
Stanford University Press.

Case Studies in Fanaticism

The Crusades

Riley-Smith, J. (2005). The Crusades: A history (3rd ed.). Yale
University Press.

Nazi Propaganda

Kershaw, I. (2001). The "Hitler myth": Image and reality in
the Third Reich. Oxford University Press.

Salem Witch Trials

Breslaw, E. G. (1996). Tituba, reluctant witch of Salem:
Devilish Indians and Puritan fantasies. NYU Press.

Psychology of Fanaticism

Nickerson, R. S. (1998). Confirmation bias: A ubiquitous phenomenon in many guises. Review of General Psychology, 2 (2), 175–220. https://doi.org/10.1037/1089-2680.2.2.175

Haslam, S. A., & Reicher, S. D. (2012). Contesting the "nature" of conformity: What Milgram and Zimbardo's studies really show.

PLoS Biology, 10 (11), e1001426. https://doi.org/10.1371/journal.pbio.1001426

Fear, Education, & Propaganda

Pinker, S. (2018). Enlightenment now: The case for reason, science, humanism, and progress. Viking.

UNESCO. (2021). Media and information literacy curriculum for educators and learners. https://unesdoc.unesco.org/ark:/48223/pf0000377068

Van Bavel, J. J., & Pereira, A. (2018). The partisan brain: An identity-based model of political belief. *Trends in Cognitive Sciences, 22*(3), 213–224. https://doi.org/10.1016/j.tics.2018.01.004

Modern Examples & Digital Amplification

Benkler, Y., Faris, R., & Roberts, H. (2018). Network propaganda: Manipulation, disinformation, and radicalization in American politics. Oxford University Press.

Rosenberg, M., & Dance, G. J. X. (2021, January 19). How Trump's election lies left a path of mutilated truth. The New York Times. https://www.nytimes.com/2021/01/19/us/politics/trump-election-lies.html

Solutions & Critical Thinking

Cerf, V. G. (2022). The internet is for everyone—but it won't be if we don't defend it. Communications of the ACM, 65 (3), 7. https://doi.org/10.1145/3513000

Paul, R., & Elder, L. (2020). The miniature guide to critical thinking: Concepts and tools (9th ed.). Foundation for **Critical Thinking.**

Additional Key Sources

Nussbaum, M. C. (2018). The monarchy of fear: A philosopher looks at our political crisis. Simon & Schuster.

Sunstein, C. R. (2017). *#Republic: Divided democracy in the age of social media*. Princeton University Press.

Chapter 14

Historical Foundations of Commodified Ignorance

Oreskes, N., & Conway, E. M. (2010). Merchants of doubt: How a handful of scientists obscured the truth on issues from tobacco smoke to climate change. Bloomsbury Press.

U.S. Food and Drug Administration. (2021). Milestones in U.S. food and drug law history. https://www.fda.gov/about-fda/fdas-evolving-regulatory-powers/milestones-us-food-and-drug-law-history

Campbell, W. J. (2001). *Yellow journalism: Puncturing the myths, defining the legacies*. Praeger.

Media, Clickbait, & Entertainment

Tandoc, E. C., Lim, Z. W., & Ling, R. (2018). Defining "fake news": A typology of scholarly definitions. *Digital Journalism, 6*(2), 137–153. https://doi.org/10.1080/21670811.2017.1360143

Barker, M., & Petley, J. (Eds.). (2020). Ill effects: The media/violence debate (3rd ed.). Routledge.

Marwick, A., & Lewis, R. (2017). Media manipulation and disinformation online. Data & Society. https://datasociety.net/library/media-manipulation-and-disinfo/

Advertising & Pseudoscience

Kozinets, R. V. (2010). Netnography: Doing ethnographic research online. SAGE Publications.

Lupia, A., & Matsusaka, J. G. (2004). Direct democracy: New approaches to old questions. Annual Review of Political Science, 7, 463–482. https://doi.org/10.1146/annurev.polisci.7.012003.104730

Cadwalladr, C., & Graham-Harrison, E. (2018, March 17). Revealed: 50 million Facebook profiles harvested for Cambridge Analytica in major data breach. The Guardian. https://www.theguardian.com/news/2018/mar/17/cambridge-analytica-facebook-influence-us-election

Consequences: Public Health & Democracy

Pew Research Center. (2019). Americans and digital knowledge. https://www.pewresearch.org/internet/2019/10/09/americans-and-digital-knowledge/

Stern, N. (2023). The economics of climate change: The Stern Review revisited. Cambridge University Press.

Benkler, Y., Faris, R., & Roberts, H. (2018). Network propaganda: Manipulation, disinformation, and radicalization in American politics. Oxford University Press.

Bayer, J., Bárd, P., & Szakács, J. (2022). Media capture in Hungary: A system of sophisticated control. Center for Media, Data and Society. https://cmds.ceu.edu/article/2022-06-28/media-capture-hungary

Philosophical & Cultural Context

Asimov, I. (1980). A cult of ignorance. Newsweek, 21, 19. McIntyre, L. (2018). Post-truth. MIT Press.

Additional Key Sources

Sunstein, C. R. (2017). Republic: Divided democracy in the age of social media*. Princeton University Press.

Wardle, C., & Derakhshan, H. (2017). Information disorder: Toward an interdisciplinary framework for research and policymaking. Council of Europe. https://rm.coe.int/information-disorder-report-2017/1680764666

Chapter 15

Polarization & Media Influence

Sunstein, C. R. (2017). *#Republic: Divided democracy in the age of social media*. Princeton University Press.

Benkler, Y., Faris, R., & Roberts, H. (2018). *Network propaganda: Manipulation, disinformation, and radicalization in American politics*. Oxford University Press.

Pew Research Center. (2022). *Americans' views of social media and its impact on society. https://www.pewresearch.org/internet/2022/10/05/americans-views-of-social-media-and-its-impact-on-society/

Erosion of Trust & Shared Reality

Putnam, R. D. (2000). Bowling alone: The collapse and revival of American community. Simon & Schuster.

McIntyre, L. (2018). Post-truth. MIT Press.

Wardle, C., & Derakhshan, H. (2017). Information disorder: Toward an interdisciplinary framework for research and policymaking.

Council of Europe. https://rm.coe.int/information-disorder-report-2017/1680764666

Socratic Dialogue & Critical Thinking

Vlastos, G. (1991). Socrates: Ironist and moral philosopher. Cornell University Press.

Boghossian, P. (2013). A manual for creating atheists. Pitchstone Publishing.

Paul, R., & Elder, L. (2020). The miniature guide to critical thinking: Concepts and tools (9th ed.). Foundation for Critical Thinking.

Political Reform & Campaign Finance

Lessig, L. (2011). Republic, lost: How money corrupts Congress—and a plan to stop it. Twelve.

Drutman, L. (2020). Breaking the two-party doom loop: The case for multiparty democracy in America*. Oxford

University Press.

OpenSecrets. (2023). Campaign finance statistics.
https://www.opensecrets.org

Community Solutions & Education

Kahne, J., & Bowyer, B. (2017). Educating for democracy in
a partisan age. *American Educational Research Journal, 54
(1), 3–34. https://doi.org/10.3102/0002831216679813

Allport, G. W. (1954). The nature of prejudice. Addison-
Wesley.
UNESCO. (2023). *Media and information literacy
curriculum for educators and learners*.
https://unesdoc.unesco.org/ark:/48223/pf0000382301

Historical & Philosophical Context

Arendt, H. (1951). The origins of totalitarianism. Schocken
Books.
Asimov, I. (1980). A cult of ignorance. Newsweek, 21, 19.
Habermas, J. (1991). The structural transformation of the
public sphere. MIT Press.

Modern Case Studies

Cadwalladr, C., & Graham-Harrison, E. (2018, March 17).
Revealed: 50 million Facebook profiles harvested for
Cambridge Analytica in major data breach. The Guardian.
https://www.theguardian.com/news/2018/mar/17/cambrid
ge-analytica-facebook-influence-us-election

Rosenberg, M., & Dance, G. J. X. (2021, January 19). How
Trump's election lies left a path of mutilated truth. The New
York Times.
https://www.nytimes.com/2021/01/19/us/politics/trump-
election-lies.html

Additional Key Sources

Levitsky, S., & Ziblatt, D. (2018). *How democracies die*. Crown.
van der Linden, S. (2022). Foolproof: Why misinformation infects our minds and how to build immunity. W. W. Norton & Company.

The Cult of Ignorance

www.ingramcontent.com/pod-product-compliance
Lightning Source LLC
Chambersburg PA
CBHW032003050726

47590CB00006B/2031